Have You Ever Said to Yourself:

- I'm tired of doing all the important work myself.
- I can't find any good, responsible help.
- I've got to find a way to make more profit.
- I wish I could pay myself what I'm worth.
- I can't figure out how to save money to invest.
- I don't think I will ever be able to retire.
- I need to figure out how to earn more.
- I wish I could find more free time and work less.
- I need my business to allow me to live the life I want.
- I wish I could get my business to work for me.

Take this test to see if your business is working the way you want it to.

Yes	No	
		I like to be in control and in charge
		I have to make most of the important business decisions
		I do all the hiring, firing, and scheduling
		I am in charge of pricing, marketing, and sales
		It's easier to do things myself than delegate them
		I work more hours than my managers
		I can't find any dependable, responsible help
		I feel guilty when I leave work early
		If I'm not there, nothing gets done properly
		My staff won't make decisions without asking me first
		It's hard to get my staff to try new ideas
		I have to push people to make their goals and deadlines
		My customers call me about most important issues
		I'm not getting the bottom-line results I want
		My staff doesn't understand how to make a profit
		My staff needs to take charge and get better
		I know what I should do but I don't do it
		My business isn't creating any equity or wealth
		I never have enough time to do what I want to do
		My business doesn't work without me
		My business isn't working the way I want it to

How Did You Do?

If you answered yes to more than one of the questions above, you need to start rethinking things like your role in your business, how you're running your business, how to increase your profits, and how to draft a plan to get your business to work on its own so you can concentrate on doing what you really want to do.

The problem is simple—your business isn't working. You wouldn't be reading this book otherwise.

It may surprise you, but **the answer to your problem is simple as well:** *You need to create solid business systems*, cogs that work together to make your company's performance both predictable and profitable, over and over again, without you having to micromanage everything.

To find out how to fix your problems and find real solutions, keep reading.

Problems are the outside indicator of the inside condition of how *you* operate your business—if you're honest with yourself.

Praise for *Get Your Business to Work!*

"This book will help any business owner avoid the many mistakes most make as they grow. I wish I had read it before I founded and built my 100 million dollar company."
—Randy Crockett, founder and president, Crockett Container Corporation

"George Hedley knows what it takes to build a successful company and has a great talent for connecting with readers. The practical real-world advice in this book lays out a simple plan that separates the successful businesses from those that constantly struggle and will save an entrepreneur a ton of money and frustration."
—Wally Evans, president, Cahaba Media Group, Inc.;
publisher, *Construction Business Owner* magazine

"This book is the definitive guide to true small-business growth. George lays out what you need to know and do to meet your goals. He is a true master, and this book is right on the money."
—Mark LeBlanc, owner, Small Business Success;
author, *Growing Your Business!*

"Starting and growing my company into forty locations with 200 employees was exciting and challenging. Reading *Get Your Business to Work!* years ago would have made my journey easier, quicker, and more profitable. Whether you are just starting your company, have one location, or want to expand it to many, this book is a must-read."
—Kim Megonigal, founder and CEO, Kimco Staffing Services, Inc.

"George has done it again with *Get Your Business to Work!* I am always amazed and inspired by George Hedley's innovative ideas to building a successful company. It delivers hard-hitting, realistic steps to help business owners be profitable and well-organized. This remarkable and encouraging book is a must-read for any business owner."
—Wes and Kerry Hacker, founders and owners, Hacker Industries, Inc.

"It took us years to learn half of what George laid out so clearly in this book. His blueprint and game plan would have gotten us to our goals much quicker than we experienced. Well-written and easy to follow."
—Jerry and Bobbi Dauderman, founders, Nautilus Plus

"Every business owner must read this book. It is the roadmap to building a company that works without the owner doing all the work."

—Bill Tutton, founder and president, Tutton Insurance

"I loved the message and hands-on exercises in *Get Your Business to Work!* George Hedley understands what entrepreneurs go through—the pain and the glory, and all the issues we face! George not only pinpoints the problems; he also provides the means to the solutions. And he shows us how to find ultimate entrepreneurial success, freedom, and wealth by applying the grounded wisdom found between these pages!"

—Andrea H. Gold, president, Gold Stars Speakers Bureau;
CEO, Dynamic Pathways, Inc.

"A powerful book from someone who actually is a self-made entrepreneur—should be mandatory reading for business owners and those who aspire to become one."

—Guy Johnson, founder and president, Johnson Capital

"Entrepreneurs make a number of mistakes getting their businesses to work. This book would have assisted me in avoiding most of those mistakes. As a first-time entrepreneur, you realize that starting a business is not for the faint of heart. This book helps you maneuver your business around potential momentum-changing mistakes. One of the best resources for any entrepreneur looking to stabilize and grow his or her business."

—Paul Tabet, founder and CEO, Topline Capital, LLC

"By following George's words of wisdom, we had our best year ever and the future looks bright."

—Chuck Ciarlo, founder, president, and CEO, Monet Software, Inc.

"I wish I had this book when I founded my investment fund management business. It lays out exactly what you have to do to build and grow a profitable company."

—Jon Fosheim, president and founder, Oak Hill REIT Management

"*Get Your Business to Work!* will help every professional transform, grow, and build his or her practice into a profitable and organized business."

—Dr. Sherri Worth, DDS, Cosmetic & Reconstructive Dentistry

Get Your Business to Work!

7 Steps to Earning More, Working Less, and Living the Life You Want

George Hedley

BENBELLA BOOKS, INC.

Dallas, TX

BENBELLA

BenBella Books, Inc.
6440 N. Central Expressway, Suite 503
Dallas, TX 75206
www.benbellabooks.com
Send feedback to feedback@benbellabooks.com

Printed in the United States of America
10 9 8 7 6 5 4 3 2 1

Library of Congress Cataloging-in-Publication Data is available for this title.
ISBN 978-1933771-71-7

Proofreading by Stacia Seaman and Gregory Teague
Cover design by Melody Cadungog
Text design and composition by PerfecType, Nashville, TN
Printed by Bang Printing

Distributed by Perseus Distribution
perseusdistribution.com

To place orders through Perseus Distribution:
Tel: 800-343-4499
Fax: 800-351-5073
E-mail: orderentry@perseusbooks.com

Significant discounts for bulk sales are available. Please contact Glenn Yeffeth at glenn@benbellabooks.com or (214) 750-3628.

This book is dedicated to every small- and medium-size business owner and entrepreneur trying to build their business into a company that works without their constant input, direction, and attention. Don't give up the dream! You can do it. I did!

Also and more importantly, this book is dedicated to my incredible wife Alana, who supports and encourages me to continue my quest to do what I love to do: help business owners reach their goals.

—George Hedley

Table of Contents

Build an "On-Purpose . . . On-Target" Business!

Imagine you owned the perfect business. What would it be like? In my perfect business, I would come into the office two or three days a week. I'd check in with my managers. Review their numbers, accounts, operations, projects, and progress. Give them some coaching, encouragement, and direction. Call a few loyal customers and take them to lunch. Check on my other business ventures, real estate properties, and investments, and look at their financial statements. And, of course, make lots of money. Then I'd spend the rest of my time golfing, sailing, traveling with my wife, and doing all the other fun stuff I love to do! What do you think? Sound like a good life?

**Be a business owner, not a worker!
The perfect business plan:
Work a little—make a lot!**

When your business and money work for you, you have an **"On-Purpose ... On-Target" business!** You're an owner, *not* a hands-on, make-every-decision, overworked, underpaid supervisor and worker. And your worst problem is figuring out what you want to do next.

So, Why Are You in Business?

When entrepreneurs start companies, they're excited to be on their own, land some accounts, and start making money. They do a good job because they stay intimately involved in every aspect of their business. Then they get busier, hire more employees, get more customers, increase their overhead, and accumulate more projects to worry about. Then they get stressed out and unfocused because they're constantly putting out multiple fires. They forget why they're in business. They keep stretching, working harder and harder to make enough money to stay in business, keep the doors open, keep employees busy, and keep cash-flow coming in.

After five, ten, or twenty years, many business owners wake up and start questioning their efforts and methods. Nothing seems to get better. Their repeat customers ask them to work cheaper, faster, and better, and accept slower pay. Their employees want more for doing less. The government makes it tougher to make money. They've been in business for years but don't have much to show for their efforts except sour attitudes, tired bodies, more wrinkles, lots of aches and pains, less hair, and more stress. In fact, they've lost their passion and have forgotten the real reason they went into business in the first place—to get paid for doing something they love. Does this sound familiar?

Wealth and Freedom

Making money as a business owner is different from being wealthy. When you own a business that doesn't work, you have lots of money some days, and others you can't make ends meet. Being wealthy means having a steady inflow of cash to your bank account. Being wealthy gives you time, energy, freedom, and extra funds to use however you want: to help your family, to improve the lives of your employees, your neighbors, or strangers in need, or to give back to others.

To achieve wealth from the long-term cash-flow of your business, you have to work toward **creating financial independence**. When you continually struggle just to make enough money to stay alive, you spend all your time worrying about paying next week's bills, finding new customers, keeping your employees busy, and trying to survive. You shouldn't be working for your business—*it should be working for you.*

Wealth gives you choices and allows you to enjoy both your business and personal life. Most business owners work hard their entire lives. Yet my surveys of over 5,000 small business owners show that only one or two out of twenty-five ever become financially wealthy. Only five out of twenty-five ever become financially independent. The rest must keep working well into their retirement years, because they never stopped long enough to figure out how to fix their businesses and reach their goals. I know. I was on that treadmill for a long time.

The Entrepreneur's Journey

After graduating with a degree in engineering, I worked for four years as a civil engineer and then as a construction project manager. But, like my dad, I wanted to be my own boss. The problem was, as an engineer, I had no clue how to run a business. Nonetheless, in 1977 I had the opportunity to start a construction company, so I took the chance to make it big and work for myself. I figured it would be easy—bid cheap, work hard, and stay busy! At twenty-seven years old, I had four years of experience, $2,000 in the bank, I had just bought my first home, and the country was in a recession. It was the perfect time to start Hedley Construction!

I figured I already had all the tools required for success in construction: a contractor's license, a used orange Datsun pickup truck with 92,000 miles on it, a metal toolbox and lumber rack, a golden Labrador retriever, a ten-gallon ice chest, a big radio, a new hard hat with my name engraved on it, and a thirty-foot contractor's power lock tape measure.

I'll tell you from experience, it's pretty easy to start a business with the wrong tools. The problems started soon after my business began to "work." I realized I didn't know what I actually wanted, apart from more work and more money. So I sat down and wrote out what it was that I really wanted—for my business, and for my life.

Most business owners never become wealthy because they don't take the time to plan out exactly what they want. *They just know they want something different than what they're getting now!* So, in order to be a success, you must first figure out what you want, and then design the steps you need to take to build a business that works exactly the way you want it to.

> **The purpose of every business is to give the owner what he or she wants!**

What Do Business Owners Really Want?

I'll tell you what *I* want. I want my business to be:

- Completely run by my management team
- Organized and systemized
- A great place to work that attracts the best employees
- Built on satisfying loyal customers
- Making double the average industry profit
- Growing my equity and building wealth
- Creating lots of freedom and fun

Who wants to own a business that has cash-flow problems, doesn't allow you to take any time off, and doesn't build your net worth?

It took me nearly twenty years to understand that a business is a tool to create opportunities to give me what I want. The purpose of your business is *not* to make you miserable, consume all your time, force you to whine about your employees, make you hate your customers, and pile on financial stress. Most business owners shoot for **MORE**—more sales, more jobs, more customers, more profit, or more of the same.

MORE is what I call the "UN-TARGET"—wanting to be bigger, not better!

When **MORE** is your goal, you just get busier and more unhappy. You get used to being stressed and out of control. You chase bad business, say "yes" to bad offers, keep bad employees, and become blind to the bad reality of your situation. You continually hope answers to your problems will just appear, that an elusive "big client" or "perfect manager" or "magical solution" will materialize like a pot of gold at the end of a rainbow. **If only you had a clear written plan with targets and goals . . .**

Imagine you want to build your dream vacation lakefront home. You own the perfect two-acre waterfront lot free and clear. You have plenty of money in the bank for construction. You've hired a great architect and an excellent contractor. You're ready to start building.

At your first project meeting, you get asked The Big Question:

● ●

"What do you want? What would make this house perfect for you and your family?"

● ●

But you aren't exactly sure what you want just yet. You can't envision the finished house at this early stage. You figure you'll just get started and see where the project goes.

So what should the workers do? The architect can't design a house without input describing what his client wants. The contractor can't build a house without a set of finished plans and blueprints. And what about the budget, schedule, finishes, materials, sizes, and everything else?

Most business owners operate their business without a set of written plans. They don't really know what they want, so they take whatever they can get and go wherever their customers take them.

Think about your company. What would make it perfect for you? If you could hire a business consultant to design and build the perfect business, what would it look like?

Throughout this book are several Business-Builder worksheets for you to fill in and complete to help you get your business to work. They are all available at no charge to download for your use. To download any or all of the worksheets, visit:

GetYourBusinessToWork.com/book

Business-Builder Worksheet #1

Describe Your Perfect Business:

How would it work?

1. What would it do?
2. How big would it be?
3. What type of products, services, or projects would it be known for?
4. How would it be unique and different from the competition?
5. What type of customers would it target?
6. How much money would it make?
7. How would it make a difference in your industry or community?
8. How would it be organized, systemized, and in control?
9. What would it do for *you*?
10. Would it deliver peace of mind, security, freedom, and fun?

Get a Plan—Get a Grip!

Most entrepreneurs start their companies without a clear vision of what they want or a written business plan specifying their targets and goals, a management team, enough capital, leadership skills, or knowledge of how to run a profitable business. When I landed my first construction project, it went well because I did everything myself. It's simple when you have no overhead, no employees, only one project, and only one customer. You make all decisions, supervise or do all the work, make all the purchases, prepare all the proposals, sign every contract, and deal personally with every customer.

The problems begin when you start to become successful.

As your business grows, you work more hours. Your overhead increases, cash-flow becomes tighter, and you have to do more work to make the same amount of money. You don't have any extra time to check the details, make good decisions, plan ahead, or think. You start losing control, and quietly—or perhaps not so quietly—you panic as your business starts to control you.

You decide you have to find some good help. So you hire the most "experienced" people you can find—your friends and relatives. And *of course* this doesn't work out the way you want it to.

Next you hire an experienced manager to run part of your company, a professional who will relieve some of your problems and stress. Hopefully this will free up some of your time to concentrate on more important issues and priorities, and allow you to be far less hands-on.

But you can't let go, can you? You don't let your manager make decisions without checking with you first. You complain you can't find any good people who are accountable, responsible, or will work as hard as you. But you don't really take the time to find anyone or train the employees you have. So your problems pile up and multiply. **People are now your biggest problem, not the solution.**

And your business still isn't working.

Next, your finances begin to spiral out of control. You don't have a clue if you're making any money or where your finances are. So you hire a part-time bookkeeper, another relative or friend, who used to pay the bills at a donut store. But since you don't know anything about accounting, you are at her mercy. And you hope she doesn't ask you any questions or bother you with the numbers—you might have to confront the awful truth that you're running in circles, working twice as hard for less and less and less money—going nowhere fast.

The challenges of business ownership continue to mount.

You continually ask yourself:

- How do I get all the work done the way I want it done?
- How do I deal with cheap competition?
- How do I make more money?
- How do I get paid faster?
- How do I deal with unhappy customers?
- How do I find trained employees?
- How do I ever get ahead?
- How do I stop running in circles?

There are so many details. You get bogged down, inefficient, and ineffective. Things take longer to finish. Ever-increasing paperwork gets in the way of doing the piles of unfinished work in front of you. And you only have enough time to put out the fires that are always flaring up. You have to make all the decisions for everyone and try to do all the important tasks yourself. You are now officially overworked and underpaid.

If your goal was to be busy—you've made it!

When you're busy, you don't have time to train your employees, become efficient, make good decisions, improve customer relationships, or offer more than your competitors. So you continue to sell at low prices to compete, knowing you'll suffer the consequences later. Everyone likes you because you're operating at overload capacity, you buy lots of supplies from your vendors, and you keep your employees working overtime. Everyone likes you, except your family and friends—and yourself!

You're totally stressed out and frustrated. Your life is out of balance, your business is out of control, your company consumes your every waking moment, and you aren't making any money.

Your business is now "Off-Purpose . . . Off-Target."

> **Have you ever said to yourself, "I'm too busy working to make any money"?**

While writing my first book, ***On-Purpose . . . On-Target! How to Balance Your Personal & Business Life to Get Everything You Want***, I learned that all successful people have three things in common.

Successful business owners:

1. **Know what they want** (*their targets and goals*)

2. **Have a written plan** (*to achieve their targets and goals*)

3. **Always track progress** (*toward their targets and goals*)

Aim at nothing . . . hit it every time!
Aim at specific targets, and you'll be surprised at what you can accomplish!

Successful business owners know what they want and decide what's important.

Before you can get your business to work, you've got to know what you want it to do for *you*. What do you want? When I do presentations to business owners at conventions, they tell me their ideal business would allow them to have three or four weeks off every year to travel. They want a company run by a trusted management team that is empowered to make decisions and get things done. They want a unique and excellent product or service which allows them to charge more than their competitors. They want their company to have business systems in place that produce consistent results for their customers and their bottom-line year after year. They want 90 percent of their business to come from loyal repeat customers and clients who only buy from them. They want to make at least 25 percent annual net return on their equity. They want their business to allow them to expand and find additional business opportunities to grow their net worth. They want to be in control of their future and have time to enjoy the benefits of business ownership.

Use these ideas to make a list of what you want your business to do for *you*.

Business-Builder Worksheet #2

What I Want My Business to Do for Me:

Personal

Business

Financial

Operational

Customers, Marketing, and Sales

People and Leadership

Equity and Wealth

Freedom and Fun

The Entrepreneur's Decision

It was simple when you did all the work yourself, but now you're a business owner with customers and employees. And management isn't fun. Besides, you're a lousy manager and you can't get people to do what you want them to do. You have become the complaints department.

So what should you do next?

You have three choices:
1. Go back to doing everything yourself
2. Sit and wait for things to change
3. Work differently

To build an On-Purpose . . . On-Target business, you can't shrink your company to just you again. And you can't sit and wait for something good to happen. Your only choice is to **change the way you work.** It might seem easier to change your employees, customers, vendors, subcontractors, or suppliers. **But to get what you want, you've got to change yourself first**. Change the way you think, do business, manage, prioritize, work, and lead.

New Ways or No Way!

In 1985 I finally made a decision to get my business to work for me and without me. I had to change, and that meant implementing new ways of running and operating my business. I dedicated four hours a week to improving my business, installing systems, getting organized, writing operational procedures, and training my employees. You can too. Commit to getting organized and in-control by replacing yourself with systems. Work on setting goals, creating budgets, and fixing things that always go wrong. Work with your key managers and make it your priority to delegate as much as you can to them. Set up checks, balances, and tracking systems for every department, and focus on helping your key people become the best they can be.

If you were looking to buy another company, what would you want to know about it? You would ask to see their financials, customer logs, receivables, assets, and liabilities. You would want to meet their employees, look at their operations, and study their competition. What would you have on your list? The first thing I would want to know before buying a company would be:

Does the business work?
OR
Would I have to do the work?

I wouldn't want to buy a company where I'd *become* the company—make all the decisions, control everything, and supervise every detail. I would only be interested in buying a company that works and doesn't require me to do much, except to go to the bank and count my money.

Do You Own a Job Instead of a Business?

The problem with most small companies is that the owner plays too big a role in everyday operations. Without the owner's constant attention and involvement, the company wouldn't work and couldn't continue to do business. So ask yourself:

- *Do you own a business that can work without you?*
- *Do you own a job instead of a company?*

You want a business that is On-Purpose . . . On-Target and meets your personal objectives. To achieve that goal, you'll have to start working to improve your business so you can reap the ultimate benefits of business ownership: time, fun, freedom, profit, equity, and wealth. Perhaps you don't know the difference between an income statement and a balance sheet. Perhaps your strengths aren't managing people, finances, overhead, cash-flow, or the bottom-line. Perhaps you don't set goals, don't know how to run a business, or don't think you're the problem.

But only you are responsible for you—and the results you achieve.

Only you are accountable for your daily decisions and actions. Only you can do what's necessary and required to get what you want to meet your goals. Look in the mirror for a better view of the potential problem.

When's Your Wake-Up Call?

Bill owns a successful engineering and manufacturing business he started seven years ago. His business grew quickly to $1 million in sales with fifteen employees. Then it stopped growing and his profits began to shrink. As work began to get more competitive in his market, he had to lower his prices to keep his employees, factory, and equipment busy. He had a hard time making people accountable and getting them to do what he wanted them to do. When his company was smaller, it had been easy for him to act as the ringleader, process all the work flow, and meet with customers to keep them happy. But now he was getting tired of working harder and harder and getting a smaller return for all the energy he expended.

Bill was frustrated and called me to ask for some help. I did a survey of his employees and found out that while he had managers and key employees, he didn't delegate many decisions or responsibilities to them. He was still approving every estimate, purchase, shipment, order, and personnel move. When he started his company, he had been able to get plenty of new accounts from his customer contacts and friends. He'd had time to manage the work process and make sure everything went well. But now that wasn't happening, and his customers were demanding better prices and faster service. Bill was stuck, and his old ways of running the business weren't working. What could he do? His choices were to grow his company or shut it down. But he hadn't saved enough money to retire.

I suggested he lay out an organizational chart of every operation needed to manage and grow his business, then decide which roles he wanted to perform himself. Next I asked him to select and assign managers who would be 100 percent responsible for all the other tasks required to grow his business at least 20 percent per year. Bill decided to be accountable for business development, marketing, and sales, and to delegate all the operations to his management team. Bill's next challenge: actually changing his controlling behavior. If he only delegated on paper but continued to micromanage in practice, his company would fail. He needed to spend all his time finding new customers and creating profitable revenue to get his company back on track toward meeting his goals.

People tend to do what they're most comfortable doing: pricing services, ordering materials, paying bills, meeting with customers, negotiating with vendors, scheduling crews, supervising people, or working with their hands. **The actual bottom-line results your business achieves are the #1 indicator of your priorities**, how you spend your time, and your ability to grow and build a company. Your priorities determine the importance you actually give to customer service, quality workmanship, financial reporting, operational systems, marketing, sales, motivating employees, and your visionary leadership. If you're not getting the results you want from your business, there's something wrong! And chances are, it's not your people, subcontractors, vendors, suppliers, competition, or customers. It's you! Your bottom-line results are the #1 indicator of your abilities as the leader of your company, and that includes your ability to let go. *The answer is YOU!*

You are accountable for how you spend your time, manage, lead, delegate, trust people, and train your employees. I finally realized that to get the results I wanted in my company, I would have to make some big changes. But it's hard to change the way you always work. Eventually I had to stop saying things like: "I'm sure it'll get better!" or "Someday soon I'll finally get it right!" or "I know my company will work when I get that new operations manager/salesman/field supervisor/big job."

Here's a new way to look at your business:

Not enough profitable sales?	*Perhaps your sales systems stink.*
Not enough loyal customers?	*Perhaps your customer service stinks.*

Selling at too low a price?	*Perhaps you're not any better than your competition.*
Not enough profit?	*Perhaps your organizational systems stink.*
Can't find any good help?	*Perhaps you're not a good person to work for!*

When's your wake-up call? *Answer these questions to find out.*

Business-Builder Worksheet #3

Define What You Want Your Role to Be:

1. Why am I in business?
2. What are my current roles and responsibilities in my company?
3. What do I really want my roles and responsibilities to become?
4. What roles and responsibilities should I delegate to build and grow my company?
5. What else should I do with my company to allow it to reach my goals?
6. What's it going to take to get my business to work how I want it to?
7. What do I need to do to get my company to work without me?

Get in the Opportunity Business!

When I finally took a long, hard look at my business, we were commercial general contractors selling construction services against too many competitors, at too low a profit margin. It seemed all my customers were buying low-price and wanting things faster and better.

Ask yourself: What business are you in? Are you in the retail, wholesale, supply, distribution, service, manufacturing, professional services, or consulting business? *Or are you in the OPPORTUNITY business?*

Are you constantly looking for opportunities to build and grow your business, provide unique delivery methods or processes, add more value to your product and services, offer additional services, or be different than your competition? What opportunities do you seek to double your industry average profit, develop strategic alliances with suppliers or consultants, leverage your loyal customer relationships, engage in joint ventures, build a great place to work, build an empowered management team, leverage your equity, or seek wealth-building investments that don't require hands-on management? To get what you want and be On-Purpose . . . On-Target, you must *change the way you think about your business*.

The natural tendency is to continue doing things the same way: working hard, staying busy, hoping business changes for the better, and trying to keep forcing it to happen. But let me tell you something. The purpose of a donut shop is not to make donuts. The purpose of a printing business is not to print documents. The purpose of a plumbing contractor is not to install pipes. The purpose of a law practice is not to try cases. The purpose of a advertising agency is not to create ads. The purpose of a manufacturing company is not to make things.

The purpose of every business is to give the owner what he or she wants.

To make this happen, you must decide to change your company into an opportunity business that seeks to accomplish three things at once:

1. Business income and profit

2. Wealth-building investments

3. Freedom and balance

What do you need to do to start seeking more than a meager positive cashflow or income? Your current business structure and systems most likely will only allow you to make a small amount of profit. But if you change your focus, your business should present opportunities to seek wealth-building investments as well. This will allow you to enjoy freedom and balance in your life. Once I realized that the purpose of my business wasn't to build buildings for our customers, my future became clear. The purpose of my business was to generate income and profit, which would allow us to seek wealth-building opportunities, which would allow me to **earn more, work less, and live the life I want!**

Being in the construction business, I started looking for ways to leverage our services by joint-venturing real estate development projects with our loyal customers. We would still be the contractor, but we also invested some money to be a partner in the projects. This allowed us to start small and learn the ropes while riding the coattails of professional real estate developers. We slowly learned how to find good property, equity sources, and lenders so we could build and develop real estate projects on our own. Once we got a track record, experience, and felt comfortable, I brought on a real estate partner who was knowledgeable in banking, real estate transactions, and investments.

As a result, we made a business decision to fire our bad customers who only shopped for the lowest price. We stopped doing projects we couldn't make an excellent profit on. And we changed our overall company goal from growing our top-line sales volume to growing our bottom-line profits, building our equity, creating wealth, and finding more time to enjoy the benefits of our business and investments.

What you need is a Business $uccess Blueprint!

Building a great business isn't easy. But it's not about working harder—**it's about working differently.** It takes a burning desire to continually improve by setting clear targets, trying new ideas, installing systems, and tracking your progress. You must enjoy what you do, love your customers, not be afraid to hire people better than yourself, and let go of making every decision. To build a profitable business, you must know how to price your services profitably, track accurate costs, understand contracts, and do the required paperwork. To expand and grow, you have to market and sell, get referrals, present winning proposals, offer unique products, and then provide great customer service. To take your business to the next level, you must learn how to trust people and delegate decisions to them. Your time is too precious to waste on small details. Your customers want your expertise, not your sweat. You need to work at a higher level and invest your valuable time on strategic things instead of micromanaging employees who should already know exactly what needs to be done and what your standards of excellence are. This means that *you need to get organized and install systems* so your people can do what you want them to do on a consistent basis with little or no input.

Remember Bill? When he presented his new organizational chart to his management team, they were skeptical. They weren't sure he could really delegate or relinquish control. But he tried, and he actually did a pretty good job in his new role as company management team leader plus director of sales. As the team began to get weaned off Bill making every decision for them, they started to see the potential of the company's future, and they got excited about their new roles and responsibilities. Their first task as managers was to organize a system for their operations. In the past, Bill had directed traffic and acted as the quality control and quality assurance inspector for everything they did. Now the managers were in charge. If the company was to grow, they would have to get everyone trained to do things the same way. This would require systems and procedures, as they planned to add more employees in the future.

As his managers began to install new systems, Bill gained lots of free time to meet with potential customers and look for better ways to serve them. He also began looking for opportunities to expand the business by providing new services and products. He started asking his loyal customers to consider creating strategic alliances with his company and expanding their joint reach to larger territories and national corporations. He was on a roll and enjoying his business more than ever. Profits began to rise, his equity and net worth grew, and free time became more available. Bill's business was working!

After seven years, Bill had hit a plateau. He had built his business to the point where he couldn't grow any more without changing how he managed his time and employees. He finally realized he needed to change. *Working harder didn't pay the bills and wouldn't grow his company any more.* He had to look at his choices and determine what he really wanted his business to become.

What about you?

Are You Stuck?

Is your business moving toward giving you what you wanted when you started your entrepreneurial journey? As businesses begin to grow, they hit challenges and roadblocks, including lack of time, energy, money, people, and customers. **Many business owners get stuck** at this point. They can't let go. They feel they have to make every decision, big and small, and hold tight to the controls like a joystick in a video game. Some owners have organization and time management problems. Some don't like paperwork or accounting and leave those tasks for others to handle. Others like to get their hands dirty and do the work, but don't know how to run a business or make money.

Before small business owners start their companies, they are usually very competent employees or managers doing a great job for their boss (Level 1 on our **Business-Builder Growth Chart** on the next page). They are responsible and accountable, work hard, and dream about the day they can start their own business. Then it finally happens. They get bit by the entrepreneurial bug and make a decision to go into business for themselves. They go home one day and announce to their family and friends that they have quit their job and are going to start their own business. This is what I call "E Day." (The E is for Entrepreneur, Exciting, Exceptional, Excellent, Erratic, or even Eccentric!) After the initial shock, family members ask where the newborn entrepreneur will find the money to get started, secure paying customers, hire trustworthy employees, and—of course—

pay the bills. Without fear, the new entrepreneur says: *"Don't worry. I'll figure it out!"*

Most entrepreneurs are never content working for others. They want to do things their way, and feel boxed in following company rules and rituals. They need to escape and make their own decisions about how they want to do business, who they should hire, how many hours they should work, which customers they should do business

You can't get rich with your head in a ditch!

with, and how much money they can make. So they start their business and seek a better way to make a living. But most never achieve their goals and dreams.

Business-Builder Growth Chart

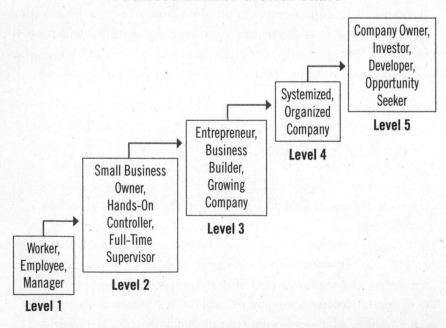

After an entrepreneur gets infected by the bug, she starts her own business and moves to **Level 2** as a startup small business owner. Here she is in charge of every decision and fully in control of every moving part of her business. She supervises each little item, transaction, customer, contact, purchase, proposal, invoice, vendor, and employee. She is a hands-on controller and full-time supervisor who approves every purchase, schedules everything that needs to get done, and signs every check. She is the boss and calls all the shots. She is a full-time operator, knows how to do all the work, and actually does most of the important work. She *is* the business. Without her, there is no business and no company.

Most small business owners get stuck at Level 2.

Some entrepreneurs remain sole practitioners forever. Others grow to two men and a truck. Some grow to eight employees at one location. And others grow to three managers and twenty employees. But when the company grows to the level where the business owner can't control everything anymore, it gets stuck and stops growing. At this point, the small business owner is unable to manage everything by himself. He knows he needs to do something different, let go, hire better people, delegate, install systems, find better customers, improve products or services, get a better handle on the process, or find more hours in the day. But he doesn't know how to do any of it. This is when he calls me and says: ***"HELP! I can't get my business to work!"***

The definition of an entrepreneur:
A person who is growing a business in expectation of
making a profit.
The key word is "growing."

A business that doesn't grow will never meet the needs, wants, and desires of a driven entrepreneur. When you get stuck at **Level 2**, you begin to hate going to work because of all the demands and pressure to get everything done for your customers, employees, bankers, vendors, and subcontractors. So what should a business owner do who is stuck at Level 2? Remember your dream of a growing business to achieve your vision and goals. At

Level 3 you get re-focused on what you want and realize again that you are an entrepreneur and business builder who wants to build a successful, thriving, *growing* company.

Are you a business owner?
OR
Are you a business builder?

As a business builder, you know how to build a company that works instead of having to know how to do all the work. You own a growing company and make that your focus and priority every day, in everything you do.

What do successful entrepreneurs have in common? How did they break through from Level 2 to Level 3 and then on to Level 4? The only way to move up to **Level 4** is to replace yourself with operational systems and get your company organized so it will operate without your constant attention. This is *the only way* you can get beyond *you* as the business. Systems allow you to get out of doing and supervising work. And with systems in place, you can then move to **Level 5** and become the **company owner**. When your role is primarily to be the owner, you'll have time to seek investments, develop new businesses, create other business opportunities, and enjoy the benefits of business ownership.

Take the First Step Toward Building
Your PERFECT Business

What will you do differently to get your business to give you exactly what you want? You *can* get your business to work. Envision your perfect company in five to ten years, working without you and making lots of money. Decide what you'll have to do to make this happen, given your people, customers, products, services, projects, money, and time. An On-Purpose . . . On-Target business meets both your business *and* personal goals. **Step one is to figure out exactly what you want.** Then you can make the changes necessary to make it happen. Without knowing what it looks like, you can't draft and design your perfect business. Take the first step by making a list of everything you want your business to be, become, do, and provide for you in the next five to ten years.

Once you have re-discovered and written out the reasons why you own your company and the real purpose for your business, write out a simple and concise Business-Builder Purpose Statement. As a model to follow, take a look at the Business-Builder Purpose Statement I drafted several years ago:

My Business-Builder Purpose Statement

The purpose for owning my business is to give me what I want!

First and foremost, I want my construction company to make double the industry average profit margin, build my personal net worth and equity at least 20 to 25 percent every year, and create wealth-building opportunities to own passive income-producing properties as a major part of our overall business plan.

I want my business to be organized, systemized, in-control, and 100 percent run by the management team. I want my company to provide excellent commercial construction and development services, deliver first-class, on-time projects, and provide full value with high integrity for loyal customers. I want all of this to happen so that I can enjoy time with my family and friends, take several annual trips with my wife, and be able to enjoy the benefits of business ownership.

My business will allow me to become wealthy, debt free, and have enough passive income to not have to seek cheap work or bad customers to stay busy. I will be able to contribute to and serve others, and still have plenty of time to give back to my family, industry, community, and charities.

Most importantly, I want my life and business to both be On-Purpose . . . On-Target!

Now it's your turn to write out your Business-Builder Purpose Statement. You can download the Business-Builder Worksheet #4 to draft your Business-Builder Purpose Statement to help you draft a concise statement of the reason you are in business and what you want your business to do for you. So do it! Get moving and write down the purpose for owning your business and what it will allow you to do. Be sure to consider these four questions:

The purpose for owning my business is to?

My business will allow me to?

My company will allow me to enjoy?

My company will give me the ability to?

What's Keeping Your Company from Being the Perfect Business for You?

Not so long ago, I surveyed over 5,000 business owners while speaking at several large national conventions. My research revealed the following.

The top two reasons small businesses fail are:

- **The owner controls everything!**
- **The owner is unwilling to change!**

If the owner thinks he or she is irreplaceable and knows more than anyone else, you get a bad business because of a bad business owner. To be successful, business owners need to constantly re-examine how and why they do things. Most companies never get to the next level because the owner isn't willing to make necessary changes. They get stuck in their comfort zone, doing the same things over and over and never changing. The company gets stuck at the same level and can't improve. What happens often goes like this:

The Downward Spiral

- Too much work for the owner to do alone
  - Hire cheap or untrained help
    - Work gets out of control
      - Customers get unhappy
        - Can't make enough money
          - Can't afford to hire better people
          - Can't find time to train people
            - No time for marketing or sales
              - Owner spends time putting out fires
              and fixing problems
                - No referrals or repeat customers
                  - Have to sell at low price to get more work
                    - Can't make enough profit to grow
                    the business
                      - No hope for the future

When I founded my company I had a pickup truck and a few dollars in the bank. Within seven years my commercial construction business had 150 employees and was doing $50 million in annual volume. Along the way I struggled with the same problems all entrepreneurs face:

- Not enough good help
- Not enough time in the day
- Not enough profit
- Not enough patience to help my people learn how to do it right
- Few organizational systems
- No freedom to do what I wanted to do

Better Is Better

When you do a good job for your customers by offering an excellent product or service, you *will* grow your business. This is both good and bad. It's good, of course, because you create more revenue, but it's bad because you get busier and busier. Then your customers, employees, and company demand all your time. You have no life away from work. You get consumed doing the wrong things. And you work too hard for the money you actually make. But your business still grows because of your intense efforts, causing you to work even more and enjoying it even less. Finally, at a crossroads, you start thinking maybe *bigger is not better.*

Your company isn't working for you; you are working for your company. Perhaps you've been there and realized that *different is better!*

But how do you build a different, more effective business? You try to work differently, but you can't change. So you continue to do things the same old way. When I wanted to fix my business I tried everything, including reading trade magazines, attending seminars, getting active in industry associations, hiring coaches and consultants, listening to tapes, and reading books. Eventually, by trial and error, through all these new ideas and a lot of grief, I discovered a step-by-step Business $uccess Blueprint to build an organized and systemized business that works for me, and can also work for you.

Step by Step

Most business owners start by trying to fix what's broken or do what's urgently needed. Business owners often e-mail me to ask for advice on how to improve their business. They ask: "Should I hire an office manager?" "How can I get my field crews to be more productive?" "How much profit should I make?" "What kind of marketing works best?" "How often should I take my best customer to lunch?" "What's the best way to compensate my employees for a job well done?" "What accounting software should I buy?"

While all of these are good questions, I can't answer them properly unless I understand what the business owners are ultimately trying to accomplish. Do they want a quick fix or do they want their businesses to grow? Are they trying to build for the future or just put out a fire? Are they looking for a quick fix or a long-term solution?

As a business owner, you have a clear choice:

Stay stuck or invest in your future.

When your business starts to grow, you can't handle all the customer orders alone, so you need to hire some good help. But because you're too busy to take the time to interview, screen, and hire the right people, your tendency is to hire anyone you can find, figuring you can train them later. So you hire the wrong people, put them to work without training, and expect perfect results.

To guarantee excellent results, you need to **create organizational systems** so your people can do excellent work the way you want it done on a consistent basis. Great people are an asset. But if each of your employees does things his or her own way, your product or service will not be consistent. You will end up with a business that is disorganized and out of your control. This will deliver poor bottom-line results *and* will cause you to be stressed out about hiring more people.

People are not your problem!

It's the lack of systems and training that causes good people to do poor work.

Karen owns a successful, growing marketing and public relations company with five employees. Her business has grown to the point where she needs an office manager to help with all the administrative duties and to run the office. She e-mailed me and asked if it was better to hire a young, inexperienced but enthusiastic secretary or an experienced, qualified office manager who had worked at an advertising agency for ten years. The younger applicant was eager to learn and would save Karen $20,000 per year in salary.

The tendency for most entrepreneurs is to hire cheap and figure you can train them in your spare time. But ask yourself this: *How much spare time do you actually have?* When you are already overloaded and your company doesn't have written systems and procedures in place, hiring inexperienced employees only makes your job more difficult. You have to do your job *plus* continually show employees how to do theirs. This takes away from your top priorities, making you less productive. Hiring an experienced professional will free you up to do the tasks that give you the biggest return on your time. In addition, a pro will be able to organize and systemize your operations for you. I told Karen to hire the best applicant she could find: bite the bullet, pay the higher price, and free up her time to work with customers and increase her revenue. She took my advice, and eight weeks later she called to thank me. The new office manager had reorganized her files, helped install a new management software package, standardized the paperwork flow for all projects, and implemented a human resources and personnel program.

Build a Better Business

When I started the process of building a better business, there was so much to fix. I didn't know where to start, and I didn't have the time to do what I knew had to be done to get my company moving toward producing consistent results on every project, with every customer, with all of our employees and managers. I finally decided to dedicate four hours per week to the task. **My business was so out of control, I figured it would probably take five years to get it on track.** But, much to my surprise, as I started to install operational systems, everything fell into place quickly and we were able to improve much faster than anticipated. We made fewer mistakes and had fewer emergencies, and as a result I found more time to work on the important issues, seek better customers, and look for more profitable opportunities.

It's important to follow the Business $uccess Blueprint. When you just try to put a Band-Aid on problems, your progress will stop. For example, I often hear business owners say: "I need to hire a good manager or salesperson." Hiring a good manager or salesperson is a great idea—once you have excellent management systems in place, including accurate pricing systems to determine the actual costs of your overhead, production, service, and products. It's a simple process of cause and effect. If you hire a salesperson who brings in lots of new business, but you don't have trained employees, organizational systems, or management controls in place, how can you make money? You'll drown in your efforts to meet the increased

demands and stress on your company. You can't grow profitably by jump-
ing ahead of your company's ability to perform. Take things one step at a
time and you'll reach your long-term goals faster. Think before you hire a
salesperson. You need to get your finances and operational management
systems in order first. Then you'll be ready for profitable growth.

What's Your HUGE Business Vision?

Now let's get specific about your vision and its accompanying targets and
goals. Part 2 of your Business-Builder Blueprint is your overarching vision.
What do you want your business to become and do in the next one, three,
five, and ten years? Think about precise targets and results you want to
shoot for and achieve. What's your vision for a perfect business? Think
about things like how you will do business, the perfect size of your company, the type of customers, where you will do business, the number of
employees, how you will generate revenue, what your company will be
known for, how much money you want to generate, the wealth and assets
you want to acquire, and what your role as the owner will be. Think **HUGE**
and be specific.

Get started now by brainstorming as many dreams you have about your
future. ***Don't hold back.*** If you want to make $1 million per year net
income or have a $10 million net worth in ten years, *write that down.*
Perhaps you want to be the leading company in your market, or the largest supplier, or have ten loyal customers who give you all their work, or
become the recognized expert in your market who charges the most.
Maybe you want your company to have five locations run by a general
manager who manages the day-to-day operations, allowing you to work on
your investments four days a week. Or perhaps you love working with customers and want to continue to be the chief salesperson and have someone
else run your company operations. The choice is yours. After all, it's your
company!

Using your dreams and thoughts identified above, it's now time to write
out and draft your **Business-Builder Vision Statement**. To give you some
more ideas, take a look at the Business-Builder Vision Statement I drafted

for my company when we made a strategic decision to transition from general contractor to an On-Purpose . . . On-Target business.

My HUGE Business-Builder Vision Statement

Within the next five years, we will transform our company into a major full-service and full-value commercial construction and development company.

As a general contractor, we will pride ourselves on meeting our customers' goals and make every project a success! Every year we will build ten to fifteen projects, generate $40 to $50 million in annual sales, and make at least $1,000,000 in pre-tax net profit.

We will specialize in building great projects for a small, exclusive group of loyal customers who demand trust, integrity, expertise, value, and terrific service. Our customer targets will include privately held corporations and professional developers, with an annual goal of 80 percent loyal repeat customers and 20 percent new.

Our project types will include: office, industrial, manufacturing, and warehouse buildings throughout Southern California. Our average project will be $6 million, and the minimum we will accept for a project is $2 million. We will negotiate 80 percent of our contracts.

We will be known for providing the best personal, professional, and knowledgeable construction services available. We will be known for our "full service" management system, competitive prices, great subcontractor relations, and accurate cost estimating. We will be known as a financially strong, fiscally responsible, systemized, organized, in-control company with cutting-edge technology.

We will also participate in the construction and ownership of at least two real estate development projects annually of at least 50,000 square feet each.

> Our company will be completely run by the executive management team. My role as owner will be to provide leadership, inspiration, direction, and motivation; set the targets and goals; keep employees focused on achieving the results we want; seek new business opportunities; stay active in the community; and not get involved in the day-to-day business or management activities.

Now it's your turn to draft your HUGE Business-Builder Vision Statement to describe how you envision your company in the future. You can download Business-Builder Worksheet #5 to help you get started writing out your vision statement.

Put Your Dreams Into Action

Now that you have defined and drafted your vision and purpose for owning your business, you can start to turn it into a working action plan. Start thinking about what specific targets you must meet to make your purpose and vision become a reality. Dreaming about your future is exciting. If you can grow 15 percent per year, your company will double in five years. If you can grow 20 percent per year, your company will double in four years. And if you can grow 25 percent per year, your company will double in only three years. But in order to keep pace with your growing company, you will need clear written plans about your infrastructure, operations, working capital, people, systems, customers, financial management, vendors, and your own role.

So if one of your top goals is to grow your company 20 percent per year, you may choose to create a Business-Builder Target like this: *Seek ten loyal customers within five years who will generate at least $1 million each in annual sales at a gross profit margin of 15 percent.* Another target you might want to achieve is to have a management team who'll run your company for you. A Business-Builder Target could then be: *Within two years, have in place a complete management team, including a general* *manager, operations manager, office manager, accounting manager, and business development manager.* Think about what targets you want to achieve over the next several years. Some will be immediate needs, and others will be things you want to accomplish over five or ten years. Be specific about the things that will make your dreams come true.

Be brutally honest with yourself. To grow your business and make more profit so you can enjoy some free time, what will you have to do differently? Brainstorm the top twenty or thirty targets you need to hit, then rank them in order of priority. Be sure to include targets in each of these areas:

Business-Builder Worksheet #6

My Business-Builder Targets and Goals

Specific Targets and Goals	Actions	Deadline
Personal		
Business		
Financial		
Operations		
Customers, Marketing, and Sales		
People and Leadership		
Equity and Wealth		
Freedom and Fun		

Put Your Plan Into Action!

After you have identified your Business-Builder Targets and Goals, think about what actions you need to take to achieve them.

Some actions you might need to take soon:

- hire a general manager
- hire a professional accounting manager
- install a fully integrated accounting software package
- get a handle on your production costs
- improve your product pricing accuracy
- find a new bank with a generous line of credit

Some actions you might need to take over the next year:

- install a least fifty written operational systems and procedures
- implement a written marketing and sales plan
- sell some of your underutilized equipment
- create a better way to serve your customers
- find an excellent project manager
- seek additional capital to grow your business

Some actions you might need to take over the next several years:

- start an employee training program
- install a customer follow-up and referral system
- create a loyal customer relationship-building system
- find a way to differentiate your services from your competition
- start an open-book incentive compensation program for all
- seek wealth-building opportunities or investments
- take more time off

What action plans are necessary to achieve your short- and long-term business goals?

Putting It All Together

Now that you've done all the work to lay out and draft your future business plans, you want to shorten it to one or two pages. This will be your **Business-Builder Blueprint** as you manage your pressing activities and decide what you should do first every day and every week. Review your business purpose, vision, targets, and action plans often to help yourself stay on track.

The Business $uccess Blueprint

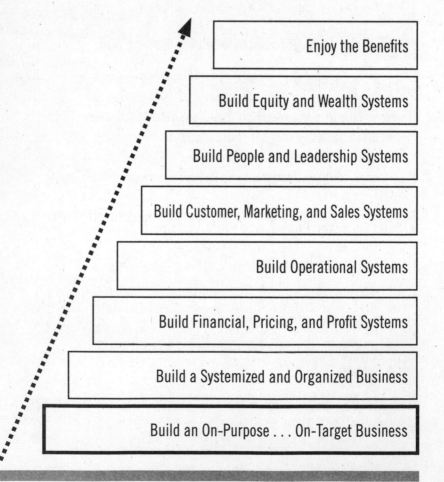

Enjoy the Benefits

Build Equity and Wealth Systems

Build People and Leadership Systems

Build Customer, Marketing, and Sales Systems

Build Operational Systems

Build Financial, Pricing, and Profit Systems

Build a Systemized and Organized Business

Build an On-Purpose . . . On-Target Business

7 Steps to Earning More, Working Less, and Living the Life You Want!

As you read through this book, you'll learn how to implement the basic seven-step blueprint for improving and structuring your business so that it works for you, allowing you to earn more money, work less, and live the life you want.

1. Build an On-Purpose . . . On-Target Business!

Determine what you want, establish a clear vision, and set On-Purpose . . . On-Target goals that are aligned with your vision and values. Identify what you want in the areas of profit, finances, customers, employees, market, service, quality, wealth, and freedom. Write goals, create action plans, and install tracking systems to make your business and personal targets become a reality.

2. Build a Systemized and Organized Business!

Replace yourself with operational and organizational systems. This will get everyone in your company doing things the same way, producing consistent results without your constant supervision and attention. Identify the systems you need and then use the seven steps to create and install systems.

3. Build Financial, Pricing, and Profit Systems!

Develop a profitable business model to give you a financial return for the risk you take. Implement the guaranteed formula to always make a profit. Calculate and track progress toward your required sales volume, break-even point, overhead, fixed cost of doing business, and profit markup to reach your goals. Install action plans to price, track, and achieve your overhead and profit goals. A fully integrated accounting system with income statements, balance sheets, job cost reporting, cash-flow projections, accounts receivable, and payables aging are required. Install financial controls to ensure accuracy and accountability. Install job cost and account tracking systems to help you determine what things really cost. Track your profitable projects to determine which products, services, contracts, and customers make you the most money.

4. Build Operational Systems!

Sound management and operations begin with a clear set of company guidelines specifying how you want to do business. Start by listing the things you want done perfectly and consistently by your entire management team, then make them accountable for getting results. Operational, administration, and production excellence starts with complete systems to ensure on-budget projects, excellent service, quality workmanship, on-time completion, and a safe workplace. The systems will guarantee that every team member produces the same end result.

5. Build Customer, Marketing, and Sales Systems!

Excellent systems to find, keep, and service customers will maximize your bottom-line by selecting the best opportunities available for your company. Create an ongoing marketing and sales program to build loyal repeat customers. Set yourself apart from your competition, find your niche market, create strong customer relationships, and seek value-added opportunities to offer your customers.

6. Build People and Leadership Systems!

Transform your job from manager to leader by implementing people and leadership systems. Change your role from hands-on controller and doer to coach and leader. This includes setting goals, motivating, inspiring, encouraging, creating a vision, seeking new opportunities, and anything else that is necessary for leading your company. Hiring and keeping good people starts with crafting a great place to work that attracts and retains the best people available. Install an employee development and training program to motivate, recognize, appreciate, and train accountable and responsible employees and teams.

7. Build Equity and Wealth Systems!

Leverage your success by seeking other business opportunities, partnerships, and ventures that will build equity, create wealth, and provide positive passive cash-flow. Use your profitable business as a stepping stone into other businesses, strategic alliances, joint ventures, and investments, such as real estate, exclusive distribution agreements, rental companies, or any additional services that complement what your company already does.

Once all this is done, you can enjoy the benefits of owning a business that works for you and gives you the freedom to pursue whatever you want to do with all your free time, energy, and money. Give back to your community, family, friends, or faith with your business success.

PUT ON YOUR HARD HAT!

Now's the time to get started building a business that works for you. Put on your hard hat, strap on your tool belt, and get ready to make your dreams a reality. Only you know what you want your business to do for you. Only you are holding it back from being what it can become. Take a look at where you are today, decide where you want to be in five or ten years, and then determine what steps you need to take to get there. Start now by taking the first step to get out of your uncomfortable zone. Let me know your progress! E-mail me your questions, challenges, and success stories. (You'll find my contact information at the end of the book.) It's an exciting journey. And the end result will give you what you want: ***Your business will work!*** **You will earn more, work less, and enjoy the life you want!**

Step 1: Build an "On-Purpose . . . On-Target" Business!

Business-Builder Action Plans

1. Describe your perfect business. (Worksheet #1)
2. Identify what you want your business to do for you. (Worksheet #2)
3. Define what you want your role to be. (Worksheet #3)
4. Write your Business-Builder Purpose Statement. (Worksheet #4)
5. Write your HUGE Business-Builder Vision Statement. (Worksheet #5)
6. Identify your Business-Builder Targets and Goals. (Worksheet #6)

To download the Business-Builder Worksheets, visit:
GetYourBusinessToWork.com/book

Build a Systemized and Organized Business!

Several years ago, I made a commitment to take charge of my company, put my priorities first, and focus on building a business that works for me. **I committed to:**

- **focus my time on important activities that produce the largest return**
- **delegate as much as possible to my employees**
- **spend 33 percent of my time with customers**
- **get home at a decent hour!**

When Monday morning rolled around, I couldn't wait to get to the office. **I prioritized these tasks into categories:**

____ **must do**

____ **should do**

____ **could do**

____ **don't have to do**

Then guess what happened at 7:30 a.m.? I started to get calls, faxes, and e-mails, which all put demands on my time. People were requesting I attend meetings, customers had issues and wanted immediate attention, project supervisors were having problems with subcontractors and needed my help, one of our crews was sitting around waiting for the ready-mix concrete to be delivered, and one of our field trucks had broken down. So I did what I always did: *I went out and tried to fix everyone else's problems for them.*

When I finally got back to the office at 4:00 p.m., I realized I had missed lunch and my desk was piled with twenty-five new requests, notes, faxes, invoices, call slips, and files—all requiring my immediate attention. So much for getting to my priorities! Then my best customer called and asked me to play golf with him at his exclusive private country club the next morning. He wanted to introduce me to his banker and talk about his next project. How could I play golf? There weren't enough hours in the day! I had to fix everyone's problems and put out all these fires in front of me.

If you're like most business owners or managers, this has happened to you. You have good intentions and want to change the way you operate every day, but you just can't make it happen.

Ask yourself:

- **What's on your Must-Do list?**
- **What's your top priority?**
- **What's your #1 focus?**
- **What will make your company successful?**
- *Do you have your act together?*

A balanced, On-Purpose . . . On-Target business cannot be built with unfulfilled goals or merely good intentions. It happens when the business owner or manager stays focused on what really matters to ensure long-term success of the company. As you observe successful and profitable business owners who have their act together, think about how they earn more, work less, and live the life they want.

Business-Builder Worksheet #7

Identify What Successful Business Owners Have in Common:

- What characteristics set them apart?
- What do you admire about them?
- What is their primary focus?
- What are their top priorities?
- How do they spend their time?
- What do they do to achieve their goals?
- What is their key to success?
- Why are they successful?
- What do they do that you don't?
- What don't they do that you do?

Successful Business Owners Live Their Priorities

There is a very successful business owner I admire who owns a large company that competes with mine. His company is continually recognized for providing the best service and quality in our field. Plus, he makes lots of money, and seems to have lots of time for his family, friends, and customers. **He surrounds himself with a top management team. He makes customers his top business priority.** *His business is based on strong customer relationships.*

I see him at the golf course every week with a foursome of well-known business executives and customers (some of them mine!). He hosts numerous customer trips to Alaska, the Rose Bowl, big sporting events, and golf outings. In addition, he takes several extended vacations each year with his family and friends to great golf resorts, and has romantic weekends alone with his wife on a regular basis. He is truly living his priorities. And his personal and business bottom-lines are doing very well as a result.

Check Your Priority Scale

When you put business pressures and everyone else first, you don't have time for the important things that make you the most money and give you the greatest satisfaction in life.

Business-Builder Worksheet #8

Determine if Your #1 Priorities Are Your #1 Priorities

Continually ask yourself:

1. Is this the best use of my time and talent?

2. Is this activity helping me achieve my targets and goals?

3. Will this activity maximize our bottom-line profits?

4. Will this activity help get my business to work?

5. Am I doing what I should be doing?

6. Am I getting a return on energy?

Take a look at where you spend your time vs. where you **want** *to spend it:*

What you do	vs.	What you want to do

It is meaningless to waste energy on doing things right,
while doing the wrong things.
Hard work alone won't make you wealthy!

The more problems you fix for others, the less they do for you. **Employees work for their boss. The boss doesn't work for her employees.** The sooner you realize the reason for having employees is to:

- get them to do what you want them to do
- allow you do grow your business
- help you to make more money
- let you to work on your top priorities

the sooner you'll start getting your business to work for you.

Accomplishing *your* priorities will make your business successful. But if you never get to them, your business will continue to struggle and you'll have to keep doing all the important work yourself.

The more *you* do, the less *they* do! The more *you* do tasks your employees should be doing, the less *you'll* make!

What Are Your Priorities This Week?

What will make you the most money and give you the greatest return over the long haul?

Business owners make the most money when they:

Have clear written targets and goals

Know their financial numbers

Spend 33 percent of their time building customer relationships

Spend 33 percent of their time leading and developing people

Only spend 33 percent of their time actually DOING work

If you focus primarily on your top priorities, you will have lots of time for the important things in your business and personal life. What will give you the greatest return today—taking a loyal customer to a major league baseball game or sitting at your computer and ordering all the materials needed to keep your employees working?

Why Is It So Difficult to Get to Your Priorities?

Dave owns a landscape maintenance business he has built up to three crews over the last few years. He is now having trouble getting all of his jobs completed every week, doing all the required paperwork, paying all the bills, and finding time to take a few days off. His personal duties include all customer contacts, sales, scheduling crews, visiting every job weekly to make sure the work is being done properly, performing tree trimming work when requested by customers, and supervising all the extra installation and custom projects. He works seventy to eighty hours every week, including Saturday and Sundays. He e-mailed to ask me to help him figure out what he can do to stop this insanity.

I asked him what a perfect schedule would be like for him. He said he wished he could have the weekends off and take at least two one-week vacations a year. I asked what he would have to do to achieve his dream. He said it wouldn't be that hard to accomplish: just take a little more time to train his foreman to trim trees the way he wanted it done, make a checklist for the foreman to follow at each customer's site, and hire a part-time bookkeeper to help him with the paperwork. Sounds simple! So why hadn't he done it yet? He had put his customers first and felt he had to see every customer every week or he might lose them. He hadn't trusted his crews or foreman to take on more responsibility. He hadn't taken time to train his workers, and he didn't know how to hire a good bookkeeper. So he put his priorities and family last.

I suggested he list all the changes he needed to make—train tree trimming, create a job checklist, hire a bookkeeper, take weekends off, and schedule two vacations—then commit to a drop-dead deadline when he would have them all accomplished. At first he procrastinated, but soon he started making progress toward his dream. Within a few months he had accomplished every task and was off on his first vacation. And, when he returned, he realized he now had enough time to go out and find some more customers and add another crew.

Make a decision to run your business like you know you should and start living your priorities. Set a date, put your priorities first, and stick to them. When I first started my business, our motto was: "Do a good job for the customer and the money will come." But I eventually realized that **when I always put customers first, I was putting myself last**. How can you truly help your customers when your business is totally dependent on you, your employees can't make decisions without asking you for the answers, you're not making enough money, and you have no personal life?

Identify things that are going well in your business versus what needs to be changed:

Things we do well	vs.	Things we should be doing better

Get Fed or Starve

Several years ago I wrote out my life purpose statement. At that time it was: **"Help other people achieve their goals."** It's awesome when you discover what turns you on in your personal and business life. It keeps you focused and becomes a beacon guiding you toward what really matters to you. For several years I worked hard as a general contractor, helping others by building buildings for them. But after fifteen years of building great projects, putting my customers first, and taking care of employees, I realized I was getting tired and worn out as my personal life was neglected.

I was giving my all in the service of others as I built my company. What was missing was the realization that *I also needed to get what I wanted* along the way. I had to change how I conducted my business and lived my life. I sat down and rewrote my life purpose statement. My new and improved life purpose statement fulfills my needs now:

If you are not moving toward achieving **YOUR** business *and* personal goals, how can you do your best for others? For example, if you work eighty hours every week serving customers, getting everything done, doing the paperwork, keeping your employees busy, and chasing money to pay the bills, your personal life will be a mess. If you

> "My life purpose is to help other people achieve their goals **SO THAT I CAN ACHIEVE MINE!**"

aren't getting a great return on the time you spend, how can you make a profit, build your business, and reach your personal financial goals? If you have to make all the decisions for your employees and close every sale yourself, how will you ever have enough time to enjoy the benefits of business ownership? If you let other people control your calendar, how will you be able to do what you want to do every day?

Business-Builder Worksheet #9

To Get Your Business to Work, Decide What You Should Do:

1. What should your priorities be?
2. How can you get the biggest return on your time?
3. What do you like to do?
4. What aspects of your company excite you?
5. What do you want to do?
6. What are your strengths?
7. What are your weaknesses?
8. What business activities should you stop doing?
9. What business activities are you best suited to do?
10. What will you do to get your business to work?

Successful business owners do what they do best and hire great people to handle the rest.

Most business owners are not very good at managing people because they think they're the only person capable of handling every task required to keep their company going. So they continue to multitask poorly, constantly performing roles they shouldn't.

When I was building my business, I thought I was a pretty good people manager. But I struggled to get employees to do what I wanted them to do. In reality, like most entrepreneurs, I was a horrible manager, and I had a very tough time making employees accountable or responsible. Because of this, my business suffered and we had significant employee turnover problems. This caused my company to get stuck as I tried to micromanage people with my controlling style. One of my biggest mistakes was not hiring an excellent operations manager sooner, which would have let me stick to what I'm good at: leadership, estimating, marketing and sales. What about you? **What business activities and roles are you best at? Which ones should you NOT be doing?**

In order to build an organized and systemized company, you've got to have a chart of your organization showing who's accountable and responsible for every part of your operation. You need a **Business-Builder Organizational Chart** to clearly define the roles, responsibilities, and requirements for running your company efficiently and with room for growth. This chart should define every area of your business and identify who is accountable. When your company is small, you will be responsible for most of the roles. As your business grows, though, you have to let go and assign key people to assume roles and accountabilities. An organizational chart will help you lay out all the roles needed in your company, along with who is responsible and accountable for what.

However large or small your company is, you need to identify every area of your operation, what tasks are needed to accomplish everything, and the roles required to build a successful growing business. Use the organizational chart I've provided as a template.

After you draft your future organization, you will need to decide what each position is accountable and responsible for. The following **Business-Builder Accountability and Responsibility Playbook** will help you assign responsibility and accountability for each position.

Business-Builder Worksheet #10

Your Business-Builder Accountability and Responsibility Playbook

Title	Person	100% Accountable and Responsible For:

President

VP Operations
  —General Manager
  —Project Manager
  —Supervisor
  —Foreman
  —Crew
  —Team Manager
  —Team Members
  —Equipment Manger
  —Service Manager
  —Production Manager
  —Production Teams

VP Pricing

VP Purchasing

VP Business Development
  —Marketing
  —Sales

Chief Financial Officer
  —Office Manager
  —Administration
  —Accounts Receivable
  —Accounts Payable
  —IT Manager

Business-Builder Organizational Chart

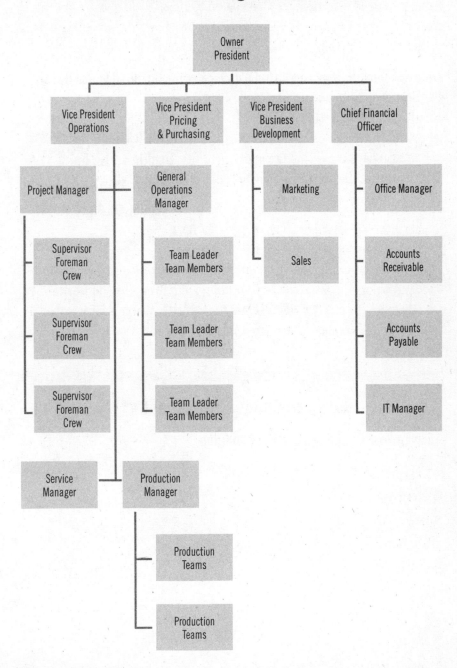

This chart will help you decide what you need to do and what you need to let go of. Spend your time on what you do best and what gives your company the biggest return. As your business grows beyond your ability to be in charge of everything, decide what position you need to fill next.

In anticipation of growth, don't hire cheap! Surround yourself with the best managers you can find, and pay them top dollar. Hiring cheap labor will stunt your growth and force you to take back the accountabilities and responsibilities you are trying to transfer to your key employees.

> **Make tough decisions! Decide to be bold! You know what you have to do, so do it now!**

What can you delegate or let go of? In order to stay focused on what will make the biggest difference in your business, step back and take a hard look at your operations. Analyze your company's strengths and weaknesses. List the opportunities for improvement and the key success factors that will make your company grow profitably, the way you want it to.

Business-Builder Worksheet #11

Analyze Your Company's Current Condition

Our Company:	Strengths	Weaknesses	Opportunities for Improvement	Success Factors
Customers				
Sales				
Marketing				
Employees				
Management				
Operations				
Systems				
Finances				

Be Bold! It's Your Company!

What should you do right now?

- Hire a key operations manager?

- Fire a troublesome employee?

- Fire a lousy customer?

- Fire a poorly performing manager or salesperson?

- Fire a relative?

- Eliminate a product or service?

- Stop accepting excuses from employees?

- Stop using the same vendors and subcontractors?

- Pay yourself what you're worth?

- Stop making all the decisions for your staff?

- Put Friday afternoons in your calendar as personal time?

The Top Two Business Priorities

In my opinion, the two most important priorities in business are *FINDING* **customers, and** *KEEPING* **customers**.

Finding customers involves everything you need to keep profitable revenue coming in the door. It includes sales, marketing, estimating, pricing, merchandising, presenting proposals, customer appreciation, schmoozing, networking, and anything else you do to build loyal customer relationships. This area is often not the top priority for most business owners. Most owners don't like sales and prefer instead to focus on getting work done. But finding good customers cannot always be easily delegated. Most customers want to know who they are doing business with, especially when they are dealing with small, growing businesses.

Keeping customers is all about doing a good job and meeting your customers' expectations and contractual requirements. This is easily achieved with an organized and systemized operation led by a professional management team and well-trained employees. The operations part of your company can be overseen by managers who implement your business vision, mission, organizational systems, and procedures. Without written and tested systems in place, delegating operational tasks is impossible, even with great people.

Hire Pros to Grow

Here's an e-mail I received from a plumbing and heating contractor from Santa Fe, New Mexico, who saw me present at a national plumbing association convention. He wanted to share some things that work for him:

Fire the idiots!

But more importantly, I found two top-notch foremen and convinced them to come to work for me. Since I had to offer them about a 50 percent wage premium over market, I had to raise my hourly billing rates significantly and charge them out even higher on bid work. Guess what? Virtually no customers were lost, my percentage of really excited customers soared, and I was free to do what I do best: sell jobs!

These foremen now run their jobs, ask me an occasional question (perhaps just to flatter me), and I give them free rein. After this experience I realized that if I have to go to a job site for any reason other than boredom, curiosity, or P.R., I don't have the right man on the job.

Find the right people, give them the right tools and direction, set 'em free, and never look back!

The fastest way to get your company organized and focused on keeping customers is to hire the best workers and give them the task of getting the work done. Great people do cost more money, but they take less time to train and manage.

You'll never be able to get your business to grow
beyond the capacity of your top people.

Where do you need the most help today?

General manager
Accounting manager
Operations manager
Sales manager
Chief estimator / pricing manager
Crew general supervisor
Project manager
Office manager

Why haven't you hired management professionals to help grow your business? Maybe you think you can't afford it right now, but when will you be able to? *Great managers will make you money.* You can't continue to do it all yourself. So do whatever it takes! Sell your car, truck, or backhoe, lease a used one, then take the money and hire a professional to help you.

Put Your Priorities to Work

Don't just talk about it, get started! Continually ask yourself whether what you're doing is a good use of your time, money, talent, or energy. When you are moving toward your goals, improving your business, and seeing progress, you will get excited about your future. What is your top priority? Stay focused on it! Always remember:

Your #1 priority is to keep your #1 priority your #1 priority!

Replace Yourself with Systems

Have you noticed that your business is a lot like a circus? You spend your days juggling, lion taming, fire eating, sword swallowing, getting shot out of a cannon, walking tightropes, dealing with clowns, cleaning up after the elephants, and working with monkeys! With today's pressure to do more with less, how can you get it all done? Where do you start?

Use the checklist below to determine where your business needs the most immediate help.

____ Technology, computers, or website

____ Finding and training good help

____ Getting paid, checking cash-flow, or making payroll

____ Dealing with customers

____ Training employees

____ Reviewing and monitoring government regulations

____ Ordering products and materials or checking on orders

____ Meeting with suppliers and vendors

____ Selling your products or services

____ Negotiating contracts

____ Working on proposals or estimates

____ Checking workmanship quality

____ Scheduling and coordinating employees

____ Keeping projects on schedule

This may seem like an impossibly long list. ***How do you get it all done and still have time to focus on your priorities?***

In 1985 my company's management team had expanded to six key people, we had ten project managers, fifteen people in administration and accounting, twenty-five field supervisors, and seventy-five men on our field concrete crews. My business goal was to have a profitable company run by my management team. But **I was still trying to do too much myself**, still trying to make every important decision. I continued to work with estimators on every bid, presented every proposal, attended every job meeting, supervised every concrete pour, reviewed every invoice, approved every purchase, signed every contract, and was too involved in every aspect of the business. I even got involved in the little decisions like purchasing office equipment, hiring, firing, tool maintenance, contract management, and what kind of coffee we should buy for the office staff. *No matter how hard I tried to let go and delegate, I just couldn't.*

It was easier to do it all myself than to trust my people. My actions drove me nuts and drove my employees crazy. It became difficult to get good people to stay at our company, as I was micromanaging and trying to control their every move. And when they couldn't read my mind, I got upset with them.

One evening I took my family out for a Happy Meal at McDonald's. When I looked around the restaurant, I noticed that the boss wasn't there, the employees were sixteen years old, customers were happy, and the food was consistent, served fast, and relatively tasty. I thought: "How do they do it without the owner supervising and making every decision?" I asked a server to show me their secret. He took me behind the counter where they have pictures clearly displaying how to build hamburgers and every other menu item. It was that simple.

Wow! **A huge multi-location company runs smoothly by using simple pictures and checklists of the finished product so it can always be done the way the management wants.** It shows employees what's expected, and guarantees consistent quality and performance by even less-than-perfect employees. Plus, the owner doesn't have to be on-site all day supervising the preparation of every customer's order. If McDonald's could do this in their company, why couldn't I?

I suddenly realized that written operational systems would reduce my dependence on finding superhuman people who could read my mind and do their work exactly the way I wanted them to do it, without my constant supervision, checking, or inspection.

Systems are the key!

I started to understand and realize that systems and minimum company standards are the key to building an excellent company. A disorganized company controlled by the owner can't grow and become excellent. It gets stuck at the level at which the owner can direct traffic and control the work flow. Systems allow businesses to produce the same results every time. With systems, you won't have one manager handling decisions one way and another doing things differently. Systems ensure that the little things are taken care of without you constantly reminding people to do them the way you want them done. Systems allow you to focus on important tasks that make you the most money. Systems allow you to deliver consistent results to your bottom-line, your customers, and your projects every time, without you being there, making every decision, and looking over everyone's shoulder.

Business owners want to count on the same thing every time! That includes every customer interaction, decision, selling opportunity, transaction, finished product, service, job, or project. You don't want to rely on people to remember what you tell them to do. Whether it's getting customer approvals or signatures in writing, following up on an order, measuring before you cut, asking the right questions before you give final prices, ordering the right materials, greeting customers, handling billing matters, checking your inventory, or filling out employee timecards, you want all of your employees in management, administration, sales, customer service, and production doing things the same way. **Systems are the only solution to get your company where you want it to be.**

Keep Systems Simple!

I've noticed that excellent companies have simple systems. For example, at hotels, all the rooms always look the same when they're ready to be occupied. How do they do this? Simple! The supervisors *show* the housekeepers what they want by displaying a clear picture of a finished and occupant-ready room. They don't care *how* the final results are accomplished, just that the room is perfect and the same as every other room in the hotel when they're done. This simple approach can be applied to every part of your business. As I grasped this concept, my personal goal became to **replace myself with systems**.

I finally realized it takes more than hiring great employees, excellent sales-people, fantastic supervisors, or magnificent managers. They were not going to make my company perform the way I wanted it to. Why? Because they didn't know what I wanted done on a regular basis. When your company isn't organized or systemized with written procedures to follow, the results are not consistent, and your company is constantly out of control, relying on you to put out all the fires and make every decision to keep the balls in the air. Without systems, even the greatest employees can't deliver consistent results without you showing them how to accomplish what you want done all the time. You're spending your time running around solving problems and directing traffic, while your company stays stuck at the same level.

> *Solid, simple written systems are the only way to build and grow an excellent company that's not dependent on you to function.*

Written Systems Will:

1. Produce the same results every time
2. Meet customer expectations
3. Create consistent employee performance
4. Get your company organized and in control
5. Eliminate operational problems
6. Increase quality workmanship
7. Improve safety
8. Help finish projects on time
9. Increase profitability
10. Maximize your return on your time

Perfect Systems Produce Perfect Results

With written systems in place, you free up time to concentrate on real business growth opportunities, like converting repeat customers into loyal customers, seeking joint business ventures, looking for ways to maximize your bottom-line profits, motivating and inspiring your people, and finding time to enjoy the benefits of business ownership.

Here is an example of the benefit of perfect systems. As a building contractor, on exterior concrete walls, you must install the door frames properly or the doors will not open or close well. At one point, we started to notice door problems on some projects, so I tried to figure out what was wrong. I realized that the frames were sometimes out of plumb and kinked, which caused the doors to not swing properly. This led to the discovery that some of our foremen were not bracing the frames properly prior to pouring the wet concrete into the door-frame forms, and the weight of the concrete was causing the frames to bend and twist.

But this wasn't the real problem. The real problem was that we were relying on our foremen to figure out how to install door frames properly. *We didn't have a company-wide system in place to ensure that these problems wouldn't occur.* The fix was simple: create a pre-pour door frame installation standard and a bracing system for everyone to follow on every project. Once we implemented this system, it saved us lots of money, time, and aggravation, as well as increasing our reliability.

What recurring problems are costing you tons of money and aggravation every year? Most company owners tell me their list of recurring problems is endless, that they get overwhelmed and frustrated and don't know where to start.

Which System Should You Install First?

The biggest problem with getting organized and systemized is finding the time to do it. It seems like a monumental task to organize and systemize your company with comprehensive procedures and operational systems! *But it only takes a commitment of time to make it happen.* I recommend you set aside one to four hours a week to begin systemizing your company. If you create one or two systems every week, you will have 50 to 100 systems at the end of a year. And trust me, it is amazing what a few systems will do for your company.

Work toward creating a three-ring binder of company systems for every important task performed in your business. Most employees only need ten to twenty systems or pictures and checklists of how you want things done consistently. This will eliminate most of the problems, crises, and fires that ruin your progress every day. And systems will free you to focus your time on priorities that will deliver the highest return, like creating more profitable revenue, streamlining your operations, or motivating employees to become better.

Fix-It List

Get started now. Put the book down and make a list of everything you need to fix. Identify the tasks and procedures you want to systemize and organize. Start with the most important parts of your business operation, those challenges and problems which will reduce the most problems, free the most of your time, and make you the most money.

Business-Builder Worksheet #12

My Fix-It List

Business Area	Specific Problem	Rank
Management		
Operations		
Production		
Employees and Training		
Accounting and Finance		
Administration		
Project Management		
Estimating and Pricing		
Procurement and Inventory		
Marketing and Sales		
Customer Service		
Products and Services		

Next, prioritize which business tasks are the most important to your company's success. Rank each problem and **make a list of the top twenty things you want performed the same way every time**. For example, consider simple but important things like filling out timecards accurately, specific ways of installing or assembling things, startup checklists, pre-proposal requirements, getting paid promptly, paperwork management, equipment maintenance, inventory control, employee training, customer communication, purchasing approvals, or sales call standards. *Your goal is to have each business operational system outlined on one piece of paper*, accompanied by a clear, understandable picture, checklist, and guideline of the end result needed to meet your company, customer, administration, installation, or project procedures and standards. The best systems are team designed by the people who actually do the job and know how to do the work best. You can download the Business-Builder Worksheet #13 to help you create your Must-Do list. Now it's your turn to list out your company's top twenty business activities that you want performed the same way and will produce consistent results.

Create a DO Manual

DO Manual

Next, you are going to draft a written **DO Manual** detailing the way your company does business. This will be a notebook of clearly depicted systems using pictures, checklists, instructions, and guidelines of your company's minimum standards, procedures, and the end results you want everyone to achieve. Focus first on the important procedures and standards that will make the biggest difference in your bottom-line. Just think, even if you can only commit to creating one documented company system every week, you will start to be very organized in only a few months.

Seven Steps to Creating Written Systems

#1) Identify Tasks to Systemize

Start with a notepad where you'll make your Fix-It List. Write down everything that goes wrong, you need to fix, or you want to systemize in your company. Keep your list handy, because problems occur and things go wrong all the time. Make sure you write them down as they occur. At your manager and employee meetings, ask your staff for help selecting the top-priority items which will improve your company's bottom-line the most. Choose tasks from several areas of your company so that each part of your business can improve simultaneously. Then make it your goal to create a written system for these items within thirty days. I recommend you make it your goal to fix at least one or two things every week. Systems should take no more than one or two hours each to draft. Remember, keep them simple, use pictures and checklists limited to one page.

#2) Assign System Teams

To help you create, draft, manage, and implement your DO Manual, I suggest you assign a person in your company to be the keeper of the systems. I call this important person (fittingly) the Systems Keeper. This person will help your system teams draft each system, formalize them, distribute them to your employees, and keep the process organized. You are too busy to try to do all this administrative work yourself! Make your Systems Keeper responsible and accountable for keeping the systems process moving, coordinated, and organized.

For each system you want to create and install in your company, pick two to four people to be on the system team. Their job is to maintain the company standards with the help of the Systems Keeper. Let the team choose a convenient time and location to work together to draft their assigned system. Drafting most systems should only take a few hours. If the problem you are trying to fix occurs out in the field, let the team meet on a job site or at the place where the work actually occurs. *Involve those who actually work within the area being systemized in the creation of the system*. For example, if you are drafting a system to install door frames in concrete walls, your team might include a project manager, concrete foreman, and the door installer who will install the finished door. Let them get together during work hours at a location where door frames are being formed and/or installed. Have them work together to determine the best way to ensure a perfect installation every time. They will decide on a standardized system of how to do the task the right way, every time.

#3) Draft Standards and Guidelines

Good systems are simple, and they use checklists, details, pictures, and diagrams of how to accomplish the desired end result. Each system will become the company standard or minimum required to ensure consistent work or expected results. The systems team should be responsible for drafting their assigned system on a single piece of standard, letter-sized, three-hole-punched paper. This will keep the systems simple and allow them to be assembled into your company DO Manual. These manuals will be distributed to all employees and used for training and implementation of the systems. As systems are added or changed, it will be easy to redistribute the new systems to be inserted into everyone's notebooks.

#4) Formalize

After each system is created and drafted, have your Systems Keeper standardize them into a formal one-page document for distribution. Use digital pictures with callouts, checklists, arrows, and diagrams clearly defining exactly how each procedure is to be accomplished or what the end result is to look like. Remember, pictures will make training much easier for your employees.

#5) Try It

Let each system team try out their system before they become company standards. This allows the team to work out all the bugs before implementing it company-wide. Encourage them to recommend changes and improvements to the formalized system so their final system will ensure perfect results every time.

#6) Train and Implement

At regular company meetings, dedicate at least thirty minutes to managing your systems. Have everyone bring their DO Manual to the meeting. Review and update your Fix-It List to select new systems to install, discuss any systems that are working well or need improvement, choose two existing systems to train and review again, and then train the new systems so that they are ready to implement. The Systems Keeper distributes new written company systems to the attendees. And then the team who created each new system presents it either to the entire company or just to those employees directly affected by it. Sometimes the best place to train a new method is out on the job site, in the shop, at the customer's office, or in a training room. The key is to train everyone and insist that everyone do the system per the company standard—no exceptions, including yourself.

If someone protests or has a better idea, let them put the item back on the Fix-It List for further revision. If you get dissenters, let them talk, and listen to their ideas, but insist that everyone follow the system while the team considers how to improve or change it. If the dissenters still resist, let them join the system team to modify and revise the system in a way that will accommodate everyone's ideas. **Your DO Manual will become your training manual.** Cover every system at least twice a year as part of your ongoing company training program to ensure that everyone understands and meets the standards.

#7) Follow-Up and Evaluate

Revisit your systems every six months to ensure they are being used properly and are working well. Continue looking for problems to fix, things that go wrong, and systems that need improving. Review the Fix-It List frequently, ask for feedback from your management team and key employees, and always look for ways to make your company better and better.

As you install more and more systems and train your employees to use them, **your job will change from doer to coach, from micromanager to leader.** You will become manager of the systems instead of controller of the work. You will be responsible for making sure the company systems are followed, and only you can make this happen. Your employees will not always want to follow the systems, and over time they may fall back to doing things their own way instead of the company standard—if you let them. So don't let them! Make sure your new systems have a mechanism to allow you to ensure that they are actually followed on a regular basis. For example, on a pre-project checklist, have a place for the manager or installer to sign and turn in a form showing that he followed the checklist. Your job now is only to make sure the forms are signed and completed on every job, account, or order. And if you start to see that your people aren't following the systems, your job is to insist they follow them, no exceptions, or they won't work for your company for very much longer. Using the example of McDonald's restaurants, if an employee doesn't want to put two pickles on every hamburger, how long will he last?

Get started now! Replace yourself with systems!

With systems in place, your people will do things the same way—your company way. This will allow you to spend your time on important matters. To get started, create a Fix-It List today, start creating and installing company systems, and you'll be organized sooner than you think. **Consider starting with some of these systems** to improve your operation, organization, customer service, production, quality, schedule, cash-flow, or bottom-line:

Financial Systems

Weekly accounts receivable
Check deposit log
Weekly cash report
Fast pay checklist
Time card procedures
Cash-flow tracking

Estimating and Pricing Systems

Cost history library
Accurate production cost system
Procurement checklist
Quote comparison spreadsheet
Labor burden schedule
Equipment cost schedule

Management Systems

Monthly management meeting agenda
Weekly crew meeting agenda
Customer approval system
Project progress review system
Budget tracking system
Administration paperwork system

Field and Crew Systems

Project startup checklist
Project close-out checklist
Quality control checklist
Production systems
Safety checklists
Work scheduling system

Marketing and Sales Systems

Customer tracking system
Customer contact chart
Monthly marketing checklist
Website update checklist
Standardized proposal
Marketing mailing program

People Management Systems

Employee training schedule
Employee review schedule
Recognition tracking system
Company meeting agenda
Individual goal tracking
Employee meeting schedule

Systems are the key to getting your business to work!

Without systems, your company will only grow as big as you can handle the workload, pressure, people, customers, and problems. This will limit your ability to make a profit and to get your business to be what you want it to be.

Step 2: Build a Systemized and Organized Business!

Business-Builder Action Plans

1. Identify what successful business owners have in common. (Worksheet #7)
2. Determine if your #1 priorities are your #1 priorities. (Worksheet #8)
3. To get your business to work, decide what you should do. (Worksheet #9)
4. Draft your Business-Builder Organizational Chart and your Business-Builder Accountability and Responsibility Playbook. (Worksheet #10)
5. Analyze your company's current condition. (Worksheet #11)
6. Start a Fix-It List to determine what needs to be fixed. (Worksheet #12)
7. Prioritize your company's top twenty business activities that must be performed the same way every time to produce consistent results. (Worksheet #13)
8. Start your company DO Manual.

To download the Business-Builder Worksheets, visit:
GetYourBusinessToWork.com/book

3

Build Financial, Pricing, and Profit Systems!

If I followed you around for a day, what would I notice? What would be your focus? Would you be spending your time scheduling employees, making sure materials are ordered, pricing products, soliciting customers, and showing your supervisors what to do? Do these activities really make you profitable and build your business?

You need to ask yourself this question before you start doing the many day-to-day tasks it takes to run your business: **Where's the money?**

Is there something else you should be doing that will make you more money and give you a higher return on your time? If so, then someone else in your company should be doing what you're doing—that's what you're paying them for.

Are you a money-maker or a money-saver?

Money-makers are focused on making money:

- Seeking profitable sales, revenue, and loyal customers
- Providing great customer service
- Developing and training employees
- Spending money where it gets the biggest return
- Investing in the future of their company

Money-savers are focused on saving money:

- Getting work done for the lowest or cheapest price
- Maximizing employee and equipment efficiency
- Reducing costs at every level of the operation
- Providing the minimum acceptable service
- Saving as much money as possible

What is your priority? Do you spend your time trying to save every dollar possible? Or are you focused on building a great company by investing in employees and customers? Money-makers make more money over the long haul. They do things that increase the value of their company, build their brand, increase their customer loyalty, get their employees to become better, and allow their company to make more money.

> *You can't save your way to prosperity, profits, and building your business.*

Let's take a look at the hotel business, for example. Great hotels are 100 percent committed to giving guests a great experience from the minute they enter the front door until the minute they check out. These hotels treat customers as guests and strive to give them what they want. Hotel managers don't focus their time trying to save as much money as possible or scheduling people based on running the most efficient hotel operation. They focus on creating satisfied customers who'll come back over and over again. This investment and customer focus creates profitable, loyal customers. It also stops customers from shopping only by price when choosing a hotel chain.

Bad motels are money-savers and do whatever they can to pinch every penny possible. The furniture is bolted to the floor, you only get one thin towel, you don't get a morning newspaper, you can't remove the clothes hangers from closet rods, the hot water is turned down to warm, and it seems like the clerk's goal is to make your life miserable. These budget motels offer poor service, average quality, and cheap prices. Guess what? This is like most small businesses. They sell low-price goods and don't have loyal customers. They also constantly struggle to make enough revenue to make a significant profit by trying to save their way to prosperity.

What's *your* business focus? Are you trying to invest in your future by developing great talent, giving customers a great experience, and offering the best service or quality? Or have you forgotten how to make money and where your money comes from? The easiest way to make money is to create it! **Profit starts with revenue**, and revenue comes from customers who are treated as clients by your employees. **Profitable revenue comes from satisfied, loyal customers** who want what you offer and will pay a little more for your excellent service or quality from your excellent employees.

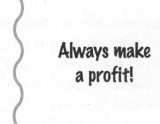

Always make a profit!

What are two main reasons to own a company?

1. Make a great profit (return) on your investment of capital for the risk you take.
2. Enjoy the freedom and benefits of owning a business that works.

Many small businesses are owned by sole practitioners who want to stay small and work for themselves forever. They like being in control of every decision, overseeing every detail, doing the important tasks, and not delegating much. Employees and customers just get in the way and complicate their daily operations. These small business owners don't really want to get bigger or grow their companies. And because they are good at what they do, they often take on more work than they can handle by themselves and with their few employees. They have made a decision to stay stuck at their level of comfort and control.

Now, there's absolutely nothing wrong with structuring your small business this way if that's what you want. But for these sole practitioners, growing their business won't happen unless they strike oil or hit the lottery. These business owners will never get ahead or earn more than the minimum required to get by. Their companies won't make them wealthy and they'll continue to be stressed out handling all the details. And they'll never enjoy the freedom of owning a business that works without them doing most of the work. If this describes you and your company, you're content with what you have, you're happy with your day-to-day operation, and your business delivers everything you want, close this book now. You don't need to hear anything else I have to tell you. For the rest of you, listen up.

Entrepreneurs want to grow their companies and create an organized and systemized business that works, is management-run, has great loyal customers, makes a robust profit, and creates wealth and freedom. The first thing you need to do is revolutionize how you think about *working*. Your company is up and running and you have people employed to help you keep it going. **Your job is NOT to do the work**. Your job is to maximize profits, seek profitable customers, and build your business.

Successful entrepreneurs invest their time:
Maximizing profits
Building their business
NOT doing the work

Successful entrepreneurs learned long ago that micromanaging people and processes doesn't result in much or enough profit. **Profit is the result of staying focused on making money so you can grow your company.** To make this happen, *you must know your numbers.* Make making money a priority. Create financial targets. Track them. And do everything possible to hit your numbers. Entrepreneurs know that cash-flow, working capital, profit, and equity are collectively the lifeblood of their future. This is what I call *profit-driven*. Most business owners are so busy keeping their customer commitments, providing the right services and products, getting their jobs finished, and keeping employees working, they don't sweat the **BIG $tuff**.

Does Penny Pinching Matter?

It is said that J. Paul Getty, one of the richest men in the twentieth century, was so cheap that if someone wanted to make a telephone call from his house, they had to use a payphone he had installed in the hall. But is this how he made his money? No. He struck oil! Most wealthy business owners got that way by spending money on the right things, making a good profit, and then investing it into strategic opportunities. Most poor business owners count their nickels, look for dimes, and keep track of the pennies, but don't want to bother with their big financial matters. As a result, these small business owners only make a very small and totally unacceptable profit margin, if any, after they collect their receivables, pay all their bills, and then give themselves a puny paycheck from the leftovers. BIG financial matters—like total sales, overhead, gross profit, net profit, accounts receivables, and cost of goods sold—*are the real reason you are in business.* Not to save every nickel, dime, and penny you can! Most businesses only make between 2 and 5 percent pre-tax net profit. **Not focusing on BIG financial matters will keep you poor**, will keep you from making a larger profit or having enough net cash-flow to grow.

Michael is the owner of a local home-improvement store, tool distributor, and equipment repair service in central Michigan. He called me looking for advice and said the economy was getting worse and his business was slowing down. "I can't sell enough products or repair services at my old markup and pricing schedule. So I lowered prices another five percent to try and attract more sales," he told me. His lower prices still weren't attracting new customers or keeping existing ones. "What should I do?" he asked.

I asked Michael a few simple questions. "What's the fixed cost of keeping your business open every month? What's the break-even revenue you need at the markup rates you're charging? What's the average sale per customer? How many customers do you average every month?"

He had no clue. **He didn't know his numbers**. His wife took care of the books and he took care of the store, ordering, restocking, sales, tools, and repairs. Odds are his wife probably didn't know the answers to those questions either, and neither of them ever discussed big financial matters in any serious way. So I politely said: **"How can I help if you don't have any idea what it costs to keep your business open?"** He said he would call me back with the answers. Guess what? I never heard from him again. I'm sure he still isn't making any profit.

Know Your Numbers!

To build a business and get what you want, you must be focused on your bottom-line numbers, know what things cost, collect your money, and always make sure you're making a profit. You can't rely on someone else to care about your finances as much as you do. You're in business to make a profit, not to work hard for little or no reward. You can have someone else pay your bills, send out the invoices, prepare financial reports, and do the accounting, but *the owner MUST be responsible for the numbers* every day, week, and month. Not just once a year when you meet with your accountant and find out too late that you didn't make what you had hoped to.

When I ask business owners why they're in business, they usually answer: "To make a profit." Then I ask: "How much profit do you make?" *Most don't really know!* This tells me that the majority of company owners don't focus on what counts most and why they are in business:

- Hit your numbers!
  - Make a profit!
    - Maximize your bottom-line!

Busy business owners spend their time negotiating with vendors, completing projects for customers, organizing employees, or making sales calls, and then hope the bottom-line numbers work out later. Often, these hard-working, dedicated people don't like to be bothered with the numbers, so they pass them off to a bookkeeper or spouse to handle, manage, and worry about. I often hear comments like: "I do the work, and she takes care of the money."

I have been an entrepreneur and business owner since 1977, worked with thousands of other small business owners, and presented keynote speeches and seminars to hundreds of thousands of business owners. My experience tells me that **less than 10 to 15 percent of all business owners actually know their numbers** and therefore continually struggle to make enough or any money. They never get ahead because they spend every day working hard to get their work done without knowing their numbers. Because of this sad reality, *only one or two out of every twenty business owners ever become financially independent.* And even worse, at least one in four businesses fails every year. Why? The top three reasons for failure include not enough profit, too little equity, and slow collections. See the pattern? Not minding the store or watching the numbers.

Basic Financial Terms

Let's start this financial discussion by defining some of the terms I use so we all know what we're talking about.

Profit is the sum remaining *after all costs*, direct and indirect, are deducted from the income of your business. This assumes that you have income or revenue and have collected it. Profit is financial gain or return from the use of investment capital in your business. This assumes you started your business with an adequate capital investment to run your business properly for several months without cash-flow problems. Profit is the remaining amount after all direct and indirect costs are deducted from the total revenue collected. **Profit is not owner's compensation**. Profit is everything that's left over after you've collected your receivables, paid your bills, and paid the owner's salary for the work he or she performed. **Profit is the company owner's reward for taking business risk.**

Without profit, your business can't thrive, grow, or prosper.

- Profit is the return for the risk you take in business.
- Profit feeds and supports business growth.
- Profit is a reward for running your business professionally.
- Profit can be split with key employees as an incentive.
- Profit can be used to help you through tough times.
- Profit allows investment in exciting new ventures.
- Profit shows you how much money your business makes.
- Profit is financial gain or return from the use of capital.
- **Profit is the #1 indicator of how well YOU run your business.**

Net profit (pre-tax) is the amount remaining after all direct costs and indirect overhead costs are paid for the year. For example, if your annual sales are $1 million, direct costs are $700,000, and overhead is $200,000, the remaining amount is your net profit: $100,000.

Profit is NOT the owner's salary or owner's compensation for performing or doing work. *Profit is the return for business ownership, taking risk,* and *investing capital* in your business.

Net profit is the best indicator of your:

- Company organization
- Management systems
- Service
- Scheduling
- Quality workmanship
- Differentiation
- Customer focus
- Marketing and sales
- Leadership
- Priorities

Gross profit is the combination of your indirect fixed overhead costs and your net profit. To calculate the percentage of gross profit, divide your annual overhead and net profit by your annual sales. For example, if your annual sales are $1 million, overhead is $200,000, and net profit is $100,000, your gross profit is $300,000 or ($300,000 / $1,000,000) = 30 percent.

Break-even point is the sales revenue amount you need at an obtainable markup rate to cover your indirect fixed overhead costs. When you know your fixed indirect overhead costs for the year, you can calculate your break-even point by dividing it by your average gross profit percentage rate to cover your overhead expenses. For example, if your annual indirect overhead costs are $200,000, and your gross profit rate is 30 percent, the annual sales you need to break even are ($200,000 / .30) = $666,666. Most companies don't reach this point until the final quarter of their fiscal year. After you cover all of your direct costs and fixed indirect overhead expenses, you can make a profit. *Do you know what net profit amount you want to make above your break-even point?*

Investment or **equity** is the most important tool business owners start their companies with: capital or cash investment. Then it becomes the total capital, retained earnings, net worth, or money left invested in your company. It includes the current equity or **net worth** of your business. At the end of each year, if you have some capital left, or it has grown, this is the **equity** in your business. **Investment** or **equity** is the net value your company is worth, or the amount that would be left if you closed your company today, cashed out, sold all of your inventory and equipment, paid all your bills, and collected all of your receivables. It does not include the extra value a potential buyer of your company might offer you for good will.

Working capital is often called **net quick**. It is your current short-term assets (everything you can sell and collect in thirty days) minus your current liabilities (everything you currently owe now and for the next thirty days). Working capital does not include long-term assets like buildings, equipment, accounts payable due in the future, or long-term receivables.

Direct costs are your total cost of producing what you sell. They include all production costs, services, materials, products, inventory, labor, supervision, project management, equipment, subcontractors, rentals, vendors, suppliers, etc., for the purchase, manufacturing, or production of the products, services, or projects you provide to your customers.

Indirect costs (overhead) are your fixed costs of doing business, whether or not you sell or produce any services or products. This includes home office expenses, facilities, utilities, general and administrative costs, rent, estimating, pricing, marketing, sales, accounting, legal, company management, purchasing, administrative personnel, support staff, office supplies, insurance, taxes, fees, professional services, and whatever else is required to keep your business open. Your overhead markup compensates for the cost of doing business.

Aim at Fixed Targets!

Don't calculate in percentages. Instead, focus financial targets by using exact numbers your managers and key employees will understand and can hit. Using the example above, the clear fixed targets in absolute annual numbers are $1 million in sales, $700,000 in direct costs, $200,000 in overhead, and $100,000 in net profit. Clear and precise!

Profit-driven owners and managers are competitive. They need targets and scoreboards. You can't win a basketball game without shooting at a target (the basket), keeping score, and knowing which team is ahead at the end of the game. You can't win a golf match without holes and scorecards. You can't reach your business goals by trying to work as hard or as fast as possible. What financial and profit targets does your company aim at?

Make sure each member of your team knows exactly what his or her targets are. Use precise financial targets as follows:

General manager   Track overall sales, gross profit, and net profit targets.

Project manager   Track exact goals for job cost and gross profit.

Supervisor   Track exact crew hour targets per week for each task performed.

Retail sales	Track average dollars sold per customer per day.
Customer service	Track customer conversion per contact.
Accounting	Track monthly deadlines for invoicing and getting paid.

Other important financial numbers to track include which customers owe you money and how fast you get paid. This is your **accounts receivables aging**. By tracking your receivables, your focus should be on getting paid faster. Also target your annual fixed overhead and net profit goal. This is your **annual gross profit goal**. Then what's left over, the amount remaining after you collect all your receivables and pay your direct costs and overhead expenses, is your net profit. Make a clear, specific **net profit goal** before you start your year. Another important target to shoot for is how much you want your net worth or company equity to grow every year. You should aim at a minimum growth of 15 percent annually and shoot for a more attractive target of 25 percent growth. This is your **annual equity growth goal**.

Are You Profit-Driven? True or False:

	True	False
I know our profit targets on every product, service, or project		
I know our annual fixed overhead costs		
I know our annual break-even revenue		
I know our year-to-date net profit		
I know our current accounts receivables aging		
I know our annual gross profit goal		
I know our annual net profit goal		
I know how much cash we have in the bank		
I know what our company working capital is		

	True	False
I know what our company equity is		
I know our annual equity growth goal		
I know our contract or work backlog balance		
I know the total and current debt we owe		
I know our exact labor, material, and equipment costs		
I know our total annual sales goal		
I know and keep track of the numbers every week		

How Did You Do?

Profit-driven business owners should have at least twelve true answers.
If you answered "true" less than ten times, you are not focused on making a profit. Your priorities are on surviving or keeping busy, getting work completed, and then getting more sales so you can continue to pay your bills and keep it going. You probably let someone else worry about the numbers except once a year at tax time. But take heart! Ninety percent of your competitors don't have a clue where they stand on most of their important financial targets, don't know their actual costs, and don't really know how to mark up their products and services so they can make a profit either. Therefore they offer their products or services too cheap. Do you know your numbers and how to make a profit?

You can't get your business to grow without making a substantial profit.

Profit allows you to build your company. I believe accountants often give business owners bad advice when they tell their clients to try and make little money or no taxable income to avoid taxes. This ongoing tactic depletes all the cash from your company and leaves you with nothing to invest to grow your business, build a management team, train your employees, develop customer relationships, or improve your product or service. The more profit you make, the more cash you have to spend on your future, and the faster you can grow and build your company. Profit allows you to invest in people, systems, equipment, training, customer service, marketing, and technology. Without a good net profit margin at year end, your business will struggle and you won't be able to move toward achieving your long-term goals of earning more, working less, and living the life you want.

Are You Addicted to Volume?

Many business owners focus on maintaining enough sales volume to stay busy. They go for *more* sales instead of *better* or *more profitable* sales. They take what comes in the door and compete against too many cheap competitors who don't know how to make a profit. They also don't offer anything much different than their competitors, so they continue to sell at low prices to stay open for business or keep busy. This causes them to take on lesser quality products, tougher customers, and work at too low a margin to cover their actual costs.

> **Focusing only on volume keeps you on a treadmill going nowhere.**

Focusing on volume eventually results in not enough profit to sustain business growth. I am not impressed with company owners who brag about how busy or how big they are, or how many employees or the number of locations they have. I want to know how much profit they are making!

Your goal is NOT to be busy. Your goal is to make a HUGE profit! So get focused on profit-building!

> *When pricing products, services, or projects:*
>
> **Can you cut your direct costs?** **Not much!**
>
> **Can you cut your overhead?** **No!**
>
> *If all else is equal, what's the only variable to profitability?*
>
> **The final sales price!**

Profit-driven business owners focus on seeking highly profitable customers, clients, projects, ventures, systems, methods, differentiating factors, and opportunities to sell their products and services. These efforts give you the highest return on your time, energy, people, resources, and your company. Profitability starts with sales. Controlling costs, expenses, quality, and purchases are easy. Selling is hard! Rather than devoting your time to daily operations, **focus at least 25 percent of your time on finding and keeping profitable customers, clients, projects, ventures, and systems, and looking for opportunities for better profit margins.**

The Key to Being Profit-Driven

Profit-driven business owners and managers know what they want. They want to make a big profit! They want to make at least double the industry average. So to make lots of money, *making money has to be your top priority!* You need precise profit targets and clear financial goals for your people, projects, products, services, and customers. Shoot for a specific return on equity and on your sales efforts, marketing, advertising, customers, services, products, time, and energy. For example, if your marketing plan calls for a half-page Yellow Pages advertisement plus an ongoing monthly outbound direct-mail campaign, keep track of the return you get for the dollars you invest in this marketing. For every customer inquiry, ask where they heard about your company. Track these calls and see how many convert to actual customers. Then you can determine where you get the biggest bang for your marketing buck.

Identify the type of clients, customers, products, projects, products, or services you excel at, the market in which you flourish, the maximum and minimum project, order, and customer sizes you manage best, and your own capacity as a company and business owner. **Decide when to say "Yes!" to a project, and, more importantly, decide when to say "No!"** That's the key to being profit-driven.

Another way to track returns on sales is to make a list of your top customers and rank them by sales revenue and net profit per customer. Then look at your sales and marketing budget and efforts. Did your marketing money get the return you expected or wanted? Should you take another look at how you spend your money? Decide which customers need more attention and how you can get a bigger return on the marketing money you invest to maintain customer relationships and increase your net profit potential.

For my first ten years in business as a commercial general contractor, I was focused on getting work and getting projects built. I grew my business fast as I focused on building sales and customer relationships. Not a bad thing to focus on. But my net profit margin was only around 2 or 3 percent pre-tax net profit—the national average for construction companies. Why?

It's easy to stay busy selling low price.

After ten years, I finally took a hard look at my bottom-line results. I realized this profit margin was too low for the risk we were taking. At a very low net profit rate, we would never be able to get our business where I wanted it to be. I was stuck in a rut offering the same things as our competitors over and over: same services, same delivery systems, same professionalism, same quality, same customer service, same proposals. We weren't any different than our competitors, so we had to compete on price. ***To make a HUGE PROFIT and get what I wanted, we made a strategic decision to work differently. We re-built our company to:***

> ***Function without me doing most of the work***

> ***Create loyal instead of repeat customers***

> ***Make double the industry average net profit***

Offer a unique, different service customers wanted

Build equity and create wealth

Give me time to seek strategic business opportunities

By changing my focus (and the company's) to achieve what I wanted, plus striving to make HUGE profits, our company had to make drastic changes in the way we did business—and earn a lot more money. We had to find different customers, use different delivery methods, develop a different business plan, and offer different value propositions. We redesigned our company and implemented major changes. **This allowed us to eventually make 500 percent more net profit** than we were making by doing business the same way we had done it for ten years.

A graduate of my two-day Profit-Builder Circle roundtable academy program wrote me this great testimonial:

I wanted to drop a line almost three years after having participated in your program. Profit, profit, profit . . . I practice and preach the principle constantly. We've become much more efficient at identifying loser jobs and clients and removing them from our midst. In the last three years we have increased our net profit to $900,000 on $9,500,000 in revenue after capitalizing $350,000 worth of equipment. We paid off $250,000 worth of debt. I paid myself a solid salary, and I've managed to acquire another property, which my company pays for in rent. I've taken at least six weeks off each year. In addition, my kids actually know who I am, and my wife no longer works in the office and is able to be a full-time wife and mother.

Now is the time to dig in and get in the profit-building business—exclusively. Forget your old ways of doing business. Give up what you are comfortable doing. Seek new and different projects, services, products, customers, opportunities, managers, and employees that will make you lots of profit.

Seek opportunities to maximize your bottom-line profit,
increase your equity,
and build wealth—
instead of staying busy and competing on price.

Is your business focused on building your future or staying busy? Does your company make enough profit to attract outside investors? If you were an investor, would you invest in your own company? What bottom-line return would you want? I bet it is more than 2 or 3—or 4 or even 8—percent return on investment.

I recently spoke at a nationwide franchise company in the home remodeling and service business. After I got to know the company, I became interested in obtaining a franchise for the Southern California area. They had promised about a 55 percent annual gross profit margin. They also suggested we could easily grow our territory to $1 million in sales by the second year of operation. And with my good business skills, we could expect to grow to several million in sales in only a few more years. It sounded great! So I began the due diligence to decide if I would invest the $150,000 franchisee fee and another $200,000 working capital to get a new business venture started.

After interviewing numerous franchise owners, however, it was hard to find one who was actually making a profit after they paid themselves a salary for their role as the general manager. Many said they were making 7 to 10 percent net profit *before owner's compensation*. But after deducting their small salary for working sixty or seventy hours every week, there wasn't much left over. Most were busy and growing, but not making any real profit. **They were only making "owner's compensation"—another term for not enough pay for the work and effort performed by the owner.** I wasn't interested in only making enough to compensate a general manager for running the business. I wanted to own a business that worked without me doing the day-to-day management of the company. Plus I wanted to make a 10 percent minimum to 20 percent targeted annual net profit on sales after the general manager's compensation and all other fixed overhead and variable expenses.

Ultimately, we turned down the franchise opportunity. I didn't want to buy a job or a lifestyle business. A real business makes a real profit.

Always Make a Profit!

"How much profit should we make?" Have you ever asked yourself that question? I'll bet your answer was one of the following: "Five, 10, or 15 percent. Or more! As much as we can get!" In a recent survey of over 2,500 small business owners I conducted while speaking at a major industry convention, I learned:

- **66 percent of companies have NO profit goals**
- **70 percent of companies have NO overhead goals**
- **50 percent of companies have NO sales volume goals**
- **92 percent of employees have NO written goals**

Shoot for nothing, hit it every time!

I know I've said it before, but I'm saying it again. Most companies shoot at moving targets by attempting to make "as much money as possible" or "more than they are currently making." **"As much money as possible" is not a target. "More!"—more than what?** These are not specific targets or goals. Five, 10, or 15 percent are not clear targets either. As your sales, variable costs, material costs, and labor costs vary each month, your total net profit earned changes. Why? Your fixed indirect overhead cost of doing business remains almost the same, regardless of volume. This causes your net profit percentage to move up and down like a roller coaster.

Trying to aim at 30 percent gross profit is hard to track as your year moves forward. A specific annual sales target of $1 million, direct costs of $700,000, overhead expenses of $200,000, and $100,000 in net profit are specific, fixed targets you can shoot for and hit. Don't shoot for "More!" or

"As much as possible!" or "30 percent!" You can't hit a moving target. Do you have specific targets to shoot for and track your progress monthly?

What's your annual **sales target?** $_____

What's your annual **overhead budget?** $_____

What's your annual **direct cost goal?** $_____

What's your annual **gross profit goal?** $_____

What's your annual **net profit goal?** $_____

According to the Construction Financial Management Association study conducted in 2007, **companies that have specific strategic plans with clear targets and goals made 33 percent more profit than companies without targets.** According to the Small Business Administration, less than 33 percent of small businesses (those that have less than 500 employees) actually make a net profit every year. It's not how much you make (sales volume) that matters, it's how much you keep (after overhead, job costs, staff, and a fair salary for the owner).

Run Your Business Like a Business

The CEOs of Fortune 500 companies are focused. They get judged on two indicators of success: their stock price or company value, and their quarterly earnings or net profit.

Do You Think Like a CEO?

Are you focused on increasing the value of your company?

Do you continually look for ways to maximize your net profits?

Do you make your people accountable for hitting their numbers?

Do you know your numbers and what it takes to make a profit?

Do you look for profitable customers, markets, products, services, or projects where you can make HUGE profits?

When I present my program "Nine Necessary Numbers You Need to Know," I repeatedly learn that most small business owners do not run their companies like a business. A business has a financial plan and an annual budget with sales goals, direct cost goals, overhead goals, and net profit goals. A business pays its president/owner a fixed, reasonable salary every month (plus year-end distributions to the owner from net profit). A business prepares accurate and timely monthly balance sheets (financial statements) and income statements (profit and loss). And most importantly, **a business makes a profit!**

A business without ALL of the above is not a business. It's a place to go to work, a place to try to make some money, a place to try to cover expenses, and a place to try to have something left over to pay for the owner's lifestyle.

Start Setting Financial Goals

If you were asked to invest $100,000 in a friend's new startup business, what annual return would you want? After considering the risks, I would never invest in a new business unless I believed I would make at least 15 percent annual pre-tax profit *RETURN ON INVESTMENT*. Why? Consider the risk of owning a share of a small business versus investing in the stock market. The average stock market return in the United States has averaged 13 percent or higher over the long term for the past three or four decades.

If your company's total capital or equity is $500,000, you should expect a minimum pre-tax 15 percent net profit return on investments equaling $75,000, after overhead (which includes the president's compensation for the work performed). Remember, a 15 percent return is the minimum, not enough—and way too low to aim at for most businesses.

I recommend that small business owners shoot for an annual net profit target of 20 to 30 percent return on equity investment. For example, if your total company equity is $500,000, your 20 to 30 percent annual pre-tax net profit goal would be $100,000 to $150,000. Now you have two targets to shoot for: a minimum target of $75,000 (15 percent) and a higher target of $150,000 (30 percent). These are *specific target amounts* you can aim for. Percentages are hard to track. So pick a fixed amount of net profit to shoot for and then go make it happen.

Another measure of return on investment is **return on overhead (ROOH)**. Every year you make a decision to invest a certain amount of money in your annual fixed indirect cost of doing business. You should also expect to make a return on this investment, which is what I call return on overhead. **I recommend that most companies to shoot for a minimum ROOH of 20 to 25 percent**. But this amount is usually not enough to satisfy successful business owners. **The best businesses make 40 to 50 percent ROOH or higher**. Make the higher target your annual ROOH goal. For example, if your annual fixed overhead costs are $600,000, your pre-tax net profit goal, using a 50 percent return on overhead, should be $300,000.

Know Your Fixed Costs

Successful business owners must know the amount they will have to spend each year to keep their doors open without generating any sales or revenue. This is called your *annual overhead or indirect fixed cost of doing business*. Some call it the "nut" you have to crack before you actually make any money (net profit).

Overhead indirect fixed costs include everything you need to run your business and keep it open all year without any sales, production, customers, projects, or accounts. Think of everything you would need to spend if you owned a store and no customers bought any products for a year. You would still have to have employees to manage the operations, production costs, and salespeople waiting for customers. You would still have rent, utilities, insurance, marketing, and advertising. This is the fixed cost of owning your business.

Overhead indirect fixed costs include:

   President or working owner
   Management
   Administration
   Accounting
   Estimating and pricing
   Marketing, sales, and advertising
   Facility, office, store, warehouse, and plant costs and utilities

Technology, office supplies, and equipment
Insurance, legal, and professional
All non-production and service costs

Direct costs, or cost of goods sold, are not a part of your overhead. They include every expense necessary to produce your products or services, build your projects, service your customers, or maintain your inventory.

Your direct costs include:

All costs required to produce the finished product or service
All costs to purchase and maintain your inventory
Production project management, supervision, or engineering
All production and manufacturing employees and labor
All production and manufacturing employees' burden and fringe benefits
Production labor workers' compensation and liability insurance
All materials and equipment to produce the finished product or service
Subcontractors and vendors to produce the finished product or service

A Manufacturing Company Example

Hardhat Shade Structures is a small manufacturer and installer of custom awnings. Their annual indirect overhead budget is shown in the example below. **The owner's task is to accurately calculate the fixed annual cost of doing business**. This is the "nut" they have to crack to break even every year, including a fair salary for the working owner or president of the company. If the owner splits his time between management and production, he should split his time between overhead (management) and direct costs (production).

Direct labor production and installation costs must include all workers' compensation insurance and liability insurance costs for these employees. These are not overhead costs as they don't occur unless these production employees are actually working on projects or services. Include all production costs into direct costs and not overhead. (Another mistake I often see is putting all of your company vehicles and equipment into the overhead. Some equipment and vehicles are used in production of the finished product and should be charged to direct costs, including their insurance, gas, and maintenance.)

Hardhat Shade Structures—Annual Budget

SALES	$3,000,000	*100%*

DIRECT COSTS
Labor

Engineering	$100,000	
Manufacturing	$300,000	
Installation	$300,000	
Employee Fringes and Burden	$200,000	

Equipment

Shop Fabrication Equipment	$150,000	
Field Installation Equipment	$100,000	
Materials	$850,000	
Subcontractors	$100,000	

TOTAL DIRECT COSTS	**$2,100,000**	*70% on Sales*

INDIRECT OVERHEAD COSTS
Salaries

President/Owner	$95,000
Management	$70,000
Estimating and Pricing	$50,000
Administrative	$40,000
Accounting	$40,000
Sales and Marketing	$70,000
Employee Fringes and Burden	$50,000

Vehicles

Management	$10,000
Facility, Rent, and Utilities	$40,000
Office Supplies and Equipment	$10,000
Telephone, Shipping, and Postage	$10,000
Estimating and Bid Expenses	$5,000
Marketing and Promotion Expenses	$25,000
Insurance	$20,000
Interest and Banking	$10,000
Accounting, Legal, and Professional	$10,000
Technology	$10,000
Service, Closed Job, and Warranty	$ 10,000
Bad Debt and Un-collectables	$15,000
Miscellaneous and Other	$10,000

TOTAL ANNUAL INDIRECT OVERHEAD	**$600,000**	*20% on Sales*
NET PROFIT	**$300,000**	*10% on Sales*
GROSS PROFIT	**$900,000**	*30% on Sales*
MARKUP ON DIRECT COSTS		*42.86% on Costs*
RETURN ON OVERHEAD (ROOH)		*50% on Overhead*

A Service Business Example

Let's look at another example of a small residential real estate sales company to see how a pure service business operates. They have ten real estate agents who earn 100 percent of their income from commission. The office staff includes the owner/manager, an office manager, a secretary, and a bookkeeper. Each real estate agent averages $5 million per year in total sales, at an average of 4 percent commission split 50/50 between themselves and the company. The total annual real estate sales volume is $50 million, equaling $2 million in gross commissions.

Your Local Real Estate Company—Annual Budget

SALES
Salespeople's Commissions
  @ 4% average   **$2,000,000**   *100%*

DIRECT COSTS
Salespeople's Earnings @ 50%   **$1,000,000**   *50% on Sales*

INDIRECT OVERHEAD COSTS
Salaries
  President/Owner $150,000
  Office Staff $150,000
  Employee Fringes and Burden $75,000
Vehicles
  Owner $10,000
Facility, Rent, and Utilities $60,000
Office Supplies and Equipment $20,000
Telephone, Shipping, and Postage $80,000
Marketing, Advertising, and
    Promotion $150,000
Insurance $30,000
Interest and Banking $20,000
Accounting, Legal, and Professional $15,000
Technology and Website $30,000
Miscellaneous and Other $10,000

TOTAL ANNUAL INDIRECT OVERHEAD **$800,000**   *40% on Sales*
NET PROFIT   **$200,000**   *10% on Sales*
GROSS PROFIT   **$1,000,000** *50% on Sales*
MARKUP ON DIRECT COSTS   *100% on Costs*
RETURN ON OVERHEAD (ROOH)   *25% on Overhead*

Markup vs. Gross Profit

To make a net profit after paying all of your overhead direct and indirect costs, you need to know the markup and gross profit you can make in the market where you compete. For starters, be aware of the difference between **markup** and **gross profit**. Markup is the percentage you mark up your direct costs when pricing your products or services. Gross profit is the total overhead and profit you make as a percentage of total sales. See the examples and formulas below from the Hardhat Shade Structures example for converting markup to gross profit.

Direct Costs	$2,100,000
Markup (OH & P)	× 42.86%
Total Markup (Gross Profit)	<u>$900,000</u>
Total Sales Price	$3,000,000
Gross Profit (OH & P)	30%

Markup vs. Gross Profit Formulas

$$\text{Markup} = \frac{\text{Overhead and Profit}}{\text{Direct Costs}} = \frac{\$900,000}{\$2,100,000} = 42.86\%$$

$$\text{Gross Profit} = \frac{\text{Overhead and Profit}}{\text{Sales Revenue}} = \frac{\$900,000}{\$3,000,000} = 30\%$$

Converting Markup to Gross Profit Formula

20% Markup = ???% Gross Profit

$$\frac{\text{Markup \%}}{1 + \text{Markup \%}} = \frac{42.86\%}{1.4286\%} = 30\% \text{ Gross Profit}$$

The higher your markup rate, the bigger the difference between your markup and gross profit will become. Look at this chart to see the differences grow.

Markup to Gross Profit Conversion Chart

Markup	Gross Profit
200%	66.66%
100%	50.00%
50%	33.33%
30%	23.08%
20%	16.67%
10%	9.09%
5%	4.76%

Set Annual Markup, Volume, and Sales Goals

One of the best ways to determine the markup and gross profit you can expect in your competitive marketplace is to look at what your competitors charge for similar products and services. Also look at your actual costs versus the final selling price you have been able to charge based on what your company offers. Then consider what you have been charging and compare it to what you think you can get in the future. The markup you will get is a result of what you offer and the value your customers determine they will pay for your services or products compared to what your competitors charge.

Next, you are ready to determine what sales target you must hit to achieve your net profit goals. You should know your fixed indirect cost of doing business or annual projected overhead. **You have a minimum pre-tax net profit goal of 15 percent return on investment (ROI) and 20 percent return on overhead (ROOH).** *Your excellent high goals are 20 to 30 percent ROI and a 40 to 50 percent ROOH.* You are tracking the trends of your actual sales versus costs for your product sales or service contracts to determine the markup you are getting. And you are aware of the gross profit markup you can get in the marketplace where you compete. Now it's time to figure out how much sales volume or revenue you need to hit your goals.

Hardhat Shade Structures

Seven-Step Formula to Always Make a Profit (Based on ROOH)

	Low Goal	High Goal
1. Fixed annual indirect **overhead** costs	$600,000	$600,000
2. Return on overhead goal **(ROOH)**	20%	50%
3. Annual net profit goal (pre-tax) $(1 \times 2) =$	$120,000	$300,000
4. Projected gross profit (OH & P) $(1 + 3)$	$720,000	$900,000
5. Average total (OH & P) markup projected	42.86%	42.86%
6. Average gross (OH + P) profit projected	30%	30%
7. Annual revenue sales goal $(4 \div 6) =$	$2,400,000	$3,000,000

Looking at the seven-step (ROOH) formula above, the company's annual overhead is projected at $600,000. The ROOH goal is 20 percent minimum, with a higher target of 50 percent. This gives the company a low pre-tax net profit goal of $120,000 and a high goal of $300,000. This will require a total gross profit of $720,000 and $900,000 to achieve their overhead and profit targets accordingly. By studying completed sales, contracts, and services, and looking at the market trends, the company owner can then determine that, based on market conditions, they will most likely achieve a 42.86 percent total overhead and profit markup and a 30 percent gross profit margin.

For you to determine how much sales volume you need to hit your annual goals, divide the total gross overhead and profit projected (#4) by the gross profit percentage anticipated (#6). (Example: $900,000 ÷ .3000 = $3,000,000 annual sales at an average markup of 42.86 percent).

Hardhat Shade Structures

Eight-Step Formula to Always Make a Profit (Based on ROI)

	Low Goal	High Goal
1. **Investment** capital or equity	$ 400,000	$400,000
2. Return on investment goal **(ROI)** ×	15%	30%
3. Annual net profit goal (pre-tax) (1 × 2) =	$60,000	$120,000
4. Fixed annual indirect **overhead** costs +	$600,000	$600,000
5. Projected gross profit (OH & P) (3 + 4) =	$660,000	$720,000
6. Average total (OH & P) markup projected	42.86%	42.86%
7. Average gross (OH + P) profit projected ÷	30%	30%
8. Annual revenue sales goal (5 ÷ 7) =	$2,200,000	$2,400,000

Your Local Real Estate Company

Seven-Step Formula to Always Make a Profit (Based on ROOH)

	Low Goal	High Goal
1. Fixed annual indirect **overhead** costs	$800,000	$800,000
2. Return on overhead goal **(ROOH)** ×	20%	40%
3. Annual net profit goal (pre-tax) (1 × 2) =	$160,000	$320,000
4. Projected gross profit (OH & P) (1 + 3)	$960,000	$1,120,000
5. Average total (OH & P) markup projected	100%	100%
6. Average gross (OH + P) profit projected ÷	50%	50%
7. Annual revenue sales goal (4 ÷ 6) =	$1,920,000	$2,240,000

Your Local Real Estate Company

Eight-Step Formula to Always Make a Profit (Based on ROI)

		Low Goal	High Goal
1. **Investment** capital or equity		$300,000	$300,000
2. Return on investment goal **(ROI)**	×	15%	30%
3. Annual net profit goal (pre-tax)　(1 × 2) =		$45,000	$90,000
4. Fixed annual indirect **overhead** costs　+		$800,000	$800,000
5. Projected gross profit (OH & P)　(3 + 4) =		$845,000	$890,000
6. Average total (OH & P) markup projected		100%	100%
7. Average gross (OH + P) profit projected　÷		50%	50%
8. Annual revenue sales goal　(5 ÷ 7) =		$1,690,000	$1,780,000

This is a great way to determine the total sales you need to hit your annual goals. Check your ROOH goals against your ROI goals. You'll see they don't match. So the different benchmarks will give you a range of targets to aim at. Generally, the ROI goals are lower than the ROOH goals. **Remember, the minimum goal you ever want to shoot for is 15 percent return on investment.** If you can't make a 15 percent ROI, you might as well close your company, get a job, and put your money in the stock market.

Companies without precise markup, overhead, and profit goals never make enough money and probably won't make any net profit. It's hard to hit a fuzzy target that doesn't exist or moves around. Company owners who know their markup, track costs, target profit, control overhead, watch what they keep, and are organized and in control stay one step ahead of their competition. Fix your overhead, set clear profit targets, and then shoot for the revenue you need at the markup you can get to achieve your goals. Keep targets in front of you all the time. Share them with your people. Track your progress, and I hope to see you at the bank!

Fortune or Fame?

The magic of making lots of profit starts with making lots of money! Building a profitable business takes focus, hard work, and tough decisions. I am not in business to be liked or famous. I am in business to make a HUGE profit and grow my wealth. When you have a fortune, you can share it and give back to others. When you are working all the time chasing nickels and dimes, you don't have any time or money to help others or enjoy your life. As the business leader, you set the example and lay out the priorities. Focus on making a profit, hold people accountable, delay marginal buying decisions, say no to tempting jobs or potential customers that look risky, don't let people waste money, let go of your poor-performing employees quickly, know and watch your numbers, know your break-even point, watch your cash-flow, seek profitable customers and projects, be firm and tough on suppliers and subcontractors, and document every order and agreement in writing.

You know what you've got to do to make a profit. Stop the insanity of trying to please everyone, be professional, and work differently! **No profit equals no future!** When profit is your #1 business priority, you'll be taking the second HUGE step toward building an On-Purpose . . . On-Target business—earning more, working less, and living the life you want.

Nine Numbers You Need to Know

Here are nine necessary financial numbers you must know, track, and review, every week and month, even if you hate numbers and just want to do your work.

1. Know your capital investment and equity numbers!

Know your equity or net worth (the actual value of your company), not including any extra or intrinsic value for good will or what you could sell your company for on the open market. Your net worth is the sum of your total assets minus your total liabilities. It's found at the bottom of your balance sheet or financial statement. A priority of every business owner should be to grow the net worth of his or her company. If your company doesn't grow in financial value, your company is stuck, and thus can't grow, hire better employees, increase its capacity, or expand. Over 80 percent of all small business owners don't know the net value of their company. Do you? Only after you know the exact amount of your company equity or capital investment can you determine the return on investment you want to shoot for.

2. Know your overhead numbers!

Making a net profit starts with knowing how much money you need to earn to cover your fixed indirect costs of doing business, also known as your *overhead*. In my survey, I discovered that less than 30 percent of small business owners actually know their annual overhead budget. This is stupid! All business owners should know how much it costs to keep their company running. This is the break-even minimum you must cover before you make any net profit. Make it a top priority to sit down with your accounting manager and learn this important number.

At the beginning of every year, calculate the annual overhead expense budget required to keep your doors open. *You must know this number!* Track it every month to make sure your actual expenses do not exceed your overhead budget. Then trim the fat. Look at every overhead check you sign. Where are you wasting money? Look especially at your insurance costs, office supplies and equipment, subscriptions, phone bills, postage, shipping costs, employee expense accounts, utilities, cell phone bills, computer and internet costs, copy machine costs, accounting and legal services, marketing expenses, and credit card charges. (When I took a hard look at our overhead costs a few years ago, I found that people were abusing the company accounts and ordering more things than we needed.) Consider outsourcing as much as you can to cut your overhead, including payroll services, employee training, scheduling, marketing services, safety programs, and equipment maintenance. By outsourcing, you'll free your staff to take care of the important things that make you the most money. And you might even find you can eliminate at least one full-time employee.

3. Know your direct cost numbers!

Before you can price your product or services, you've got to know exactly what things cost to sell, produce, or perform. The purpose of every price estimate is to create an accurate budget of what the product, service, or production costs will be. This is your cost of goods sold, or **direct costs**. About 80 percent of business owners do not know what their employees really cost per hour. They also don't know what the finished cost of their products or services are, including the labor. This creates inaccurate pricing, bids, and estimates for one of the biggest parts of your business: your people. In addition, most business owners don't really know what their equipment costs them annually or how much they should charge per hour when it is used.

Most companies don't use accurate **labor burden rates** when calculating their employee costs. Every year employee taxes and worker's compensation insurance rates change. Plus, as your employees become older and their family situations change, their health insurance rates also change. Have your accounting manager figure out the exact cost for every employee, including all taxes, insurance, worker's compensation, health insurance, vacation, union dues, overtime, tools, training, pension, profit sharing, and any other benefits you provide. You'll find that your employee burden rate can vary by 20 percent or more for each employee. When using accurate rates for labor plus burden, your bottom-line will improve.

When you own lots of equipment you feel big and powerful. BUT, are you making enough money on your equipment to make it worth your while? Calculate the exact cost for every piece of equipment you own. For each piece of equipment, add the purchase price, interest, maintenance, gas and oil, service, tires, repairs, insurance, storage, rent, and mobilization costs over the life of the item. Divide this total cost by the total number of hours you hope to bill for the equipment over that duration. This is your real cost of ownership per hour, not including overhead and profit. Next, compare this cost with the cost of renting versus owning. Get rid of all the equipment that actually costs you more money to own than you'll get back from your production or operation. Use the money you save to buy some rental property, which will actually go up in value!

I'm sure you're busy running your company, keeping customers happy and employees busy. This doesn't allow you enough time to get enough good supplier or vendor quotes for every product you sell, project you produce, or new customer account you manage. You get stuck using the same suppliers and vendors over and over. Guess what? When this happens, your final prices will creep up over time, reducing your profits and increasing your final sales price. And when you need more products or materials in a hurry, you revert to calling your good old friend at the same supplier or distributor, getting it shipped out without taking time to get another price quote from a different supplier. How much money do you think you're losing every year on just this one big factor affecting your bottom-line?

If you subcontract some of your work, review your subcontractors and look at what they are charging. They may be charging more than they are allowed by their contracts. Subcontractors also tend to round up small extras. This adds up to lots of money wasted by project managers who don't want to play hardball. Do an audit of all subcontractor change order requests over the last twelve months. When we did this, I found a few charges that didn't even end up on our jobs, like patio cover lumber, house re-paints, extra carpeting, fireplaces, a Jacuzzi, and a trip to Hawaii! Whose lifestyle are you paying for?

Next, you need an accounting system and financial software that can help your company grow and track your costs. You need accurate reports of what each part of your company's production costs are. From these printouts, you can verify the numbers you use to accurately price new products, projects, or services. If you don't know your direct cost numbers, it's next to impossible to ever make any money!

4. Know your contract numbers!

Top service business owners know their contract numbers for every account, project, customer, or service in progress. They review how well they did in the past and how well they're currently performing. To manage your numbers, you should get a monthly report listing all of your accounts (completed and current), projects, or contracts using the examples below:

Current Account or Contract Report

Account or Contract Name	XYZ Project
Contract amount	$2,000,000
Bid gross profit markup	$300,000
Estimated final cost	$1,650,000
Estimated final gross profit	$350,000
Variance	$50,000
Costs to date	$825,000
Percent complete	50%
Profit to date	$175,000
Amount earned to date	$1,000,000
Amount billed	$900,000
Estimate cost to complete	$825,000
Contract balance	$1,100,000

Completed Account or Contract Report

Account or Contract Name	ABC Project
Start date	June 1
Project manager	Dave
Supervisor	Bill
Salesperson	Sam
Contract amount	$1,000,000
Bid gross profit markup	$200,000
Actual gross profit made	$150,000

5. Know your accounts receivable numbers!

How much are you currently owed? That is your accounts receivable number. Selling products or services, making things for customers, and performing work is fun, but putting money in the bank is even more fun! I know it isn't your favorite job to call deadbeat customers and ask for money. But if *someone* doesn't focus on collecting what you're owed, you can't continue your business for long. Stop being Mr. Nice Guy (or Ms. Nice Gal) and letting your customers control your cash-flow. You delivered the product or service, so now do what it takes to get paid. Stay focused on collecting what's owed by getting an updated accounts receivable aging report every Monday.

Weekly Accounts Receivable Aging Report

Accounts	Total Due	30 Days	60 Days	Retention
Account #1	$70,000	$35,000		$15,000
Account #2	$45,000	$50,000		$25,000
Account #3	$65,000			$55,000
Total Due	**$180,000**	**$85,000**	**$0**	**$95,000**

6. Know your liability numbers!

Create a report listing all of your debts, liabilities, and large balloon or one-time payments due in the near future. Stay in touch with your lenders to maintain good relationships. And stay on top of any due dates and pay-off requirements.

Liability and Debt Report	Amount	Payments	Terms	Due Date
Line of credit				
Line of credit drawn				
Other credit loans				
Equipment loans				
Future tax payments				
Real estate loans				

7. Know your cash numbers!

Cash is the lifeblood of your business. You need to know what you've got to work with in order to make good decisions. Get a report of your cash position every week and include the following:

Weekly Cash Report

Bank deposits	
Cash in bank	Checking
	Payroll
	Savings
Weekly costs	Payroll
	Equipment
	Overhead
Investments	Liquid
	Long Term

Once you know your cash balance, you can manage it aggressively. If you run a lot of money through your checking account every year, do you know what you're earning on your bank balance? Meet with your banker to design a program that will invest your bank balance and earn interest for you. There are many ways to invest your cash on short-term, one-, three-, seven-, and fourteen-day programs. For every $1 million in sales volume, you should be able to generate $20,000 to $40,000 in interest or investment income annually. This will take about five minutes a day. Not a bad return on your accounting manager's time with your input and management!

8. Know your sales numbers!

True or false: **less than 20 percent of all company business owners know or track their annual sales volume goals.** The answer is "true." Do you know your sales numbers? How often do you track them and what do you do every month to keep them on target? My neighbor owns a successful clothing store named Flash! aimed at teenage girls. She wants to grow her business and asked me for some financial advice. Her fixed annual overhead costs are $300,000, not including inventory or products. Like many retailers, her average markup, after discounts and sales, is around 75 percent. Her goal is to make a net profit of $100,000 per store. How much sales volume per store will she need to reach her goals? Remember the Seven-Step Formula to Always Make a Profit? Her overhead and profit "nut" is $400,000 per store. Her markup is 75 percent, which converts to an average gross profit of 42.8 percent. Therefore, the annual sales per store she will need to make $100,000 net profit is $934,580. Simple to figure if you know your numbers! She is now working to add several stores and eventually franchise the entire operation

Flash! Clothing Store

Sales Required to Hit Profit Goals

Fixed indirect overhead costs	$300,000
Net profit goal @ 33% ROOH	$100,000
Gross profit (OH & P) goal	$400,000
Average markup	75%
Average gross profit	42.8%
Total sales volume needed per store	**$934,580**

Now she knows her annual sales goals per store. Next she can track her monthly sales volume revenue to make sure she is on target to hit her annual sales, overhead, and profit goals. Unfortunately, only 20 percent of small businesses set specific overhead, profit, and sales targets for the year, and then track their progress monthly. As a result, only these top companies can make necessary adjustments to their pricing, marketing, sales, customer selection, management, production, and operations as their sales move up or down with the economy or their marketing efforts.

9. Know your profit numbers!

How do you determine your net profit markup? Are you hitting your profit goals? Do you even know what your profit target is or should be?

In my research I have discovered that **less than 40 percent of companies have specific written net profit targets**. Business owners get in the rut of providing the same services to the same customers year after year. They generally only offer the minimum required services or provide the same products as their competitors. This forces business owners to compete on price against other competent businesses, thus diminishing their opportunity to make above average profit margins. How often do you offer extra services or provide added value to your customers? What do you do to double your net profit margin? What is your game plan for maximizing your bottom-line and getting more than the average competitive markup? When you take what you can get versus focusing on how to get more, you won't maximize your bottom-line profit.

Sit down with your management team every year and *decide how much gross and net profit you want to make,* then determine the numbers you want to hit. Look at the risk you are taking to operate your business. Then determine how much net profit you want to make in total dollars, and track your progress monthly.

Sound financial management includes tracking your targets and staying abreast of your progress. To build a thriving business, make it your priority to set annual financial goals and then keep track of your progress.

Business-Builder Worksheet #14

Know and Track Your Numbers!

	Last Year	This Year	Next Year
1. Sales revenue			
2. Direct costs			
a. Labor			
b. Equipment			
c. Materials/Products			
d. Subcontractors/Vendors			
3. Overhead indirect costs			

4. Gross profit
5. Net profit
6. Average markup %
7. Average gross profit %
8. Sales to break even
9. Sales to hit gross profit goal
10. Equity
11. Working capital
12. Return on equity %
13. Return on overhead %
14. Average final gross profit %
    a. by order or contract type
    b. by account or customer type
    c. by service or product type
    d. by size
    e. by location
14. Average order, sale, or contract size
15. Volume and profit per key employee

Do you know which employee, salesperson, manager, supervisor, production worker, or installer makes you the most money? Rank your key team members by gross dollars and net dollars earned, actual profit made versus profit bid, and customer satisfaction. Rank them by who hits their budgets. Focus on how better players make it happen and what low-ranked players don't do well. Give poor players a chance to improve or get rid of them. Instead of spending all your time with weak people, spend time with your best team players who make you the most money.

10. Bonus—Give Yourself a Raise!

Most business owners don't pay themselves what they're worth. What could you get paid (including fringes) for running another similar company, as their president or general manager? Make sure you pay yourself first, every month, at least 25 percent more than what you could get on the open market. The extra pay is for the hassle, sleepless nights, and risk of owning your business. This raise and compensation package will give you a feeling of value and get you focused on bigger things. You are the owner! Not an hourly worker. Stop doing everyone's job for them. Let go of the small stuff, get good people to help you so you can enjoy the benefits of business ownership. When you think bigger, you'll look for better opportunities to grow your business.

Twenty-One Profit-Building Steps to Success

1. Keep your personal overhead low
2. Pay yourself a juicy salary every month
3. Save 10 to 20 percent of all personal earnings
4. Get out of personal debt ASAP
5. Don't spend money before you've made it
6. Invest six months' working capital as reserves
7. Get a bank line of credit for emergencies
8. Balance your annual company budget
9. Only hire the best people, and pay them top dollar
10. Make a profit every month
11. Track sales and contract backlog every month
12. Track monthly cash and cash-flow
13. Track your accounts receivables monthly
14. Delay major purchases (except technology) for one year
15. Buy an income property before your second truck
16. Rent equipment until it makes you money
17. Get out of business debt
18. Reinvest 50 percent of all profits back into your company
19. Look for outside income-producing investments
20. Give back to your community, charity, or church
21. Share your wealth with those who helped you

Now What?

O.K., I get it. You really don't like paperwork, accounting, or bookkeeping. But you have to pay your bills, balance your checkbook, and collect your receivables to keep your doors open. So what do you do? You try and pawn off the accounting on someone who's barely qualified to do the job. You get your spouse, or a friend who once did accounts payable for a donut store. This works for a while, until you finally realize you know more about your costs, receivables, and cash-flow than they do.

You finally arrive at a major crossroads for most business owners. Should you hire a professional to be your bookkeeper, controller, and chief financial officer? Or should you continue to limp along with an untrained, behind-the-times, part-time accounts payable clerk or unqualified family member managing your money? Ask yourself if your bookkeeper is the right person to help your business grow. Can your bookkeeper do more than pay the bills and send out invoices?

As we've discussed elsewhere, step one of growing your company begins with a picture of what you want. I know you want a business built on sound financial principles, systems, and controls. Step two is to always make a profit. The only way to make a profit is to know your numbers and make them a top priority. Step three is to get control of your finances. Step four is to develop and install solid organizational systems that produce consistent bottom-line results.

Hire a Financial Pro Now!

As your business grows, one of your most important hires *must* be a professional accounting manager. This is a necessary investment in your future and an absolute requirement for building a thriving company. **Without a pro managing your finances, your business *can't* reach its full potential.** Hiring a qualified and experienced professional financial manager to run your accounting department is just as important to your business growth as any salesperson, office manager, estimator, manager, production supervisor, or foreman.

A professional accounting manager knows your business and is an expert in your industry and how to make a profit. This includes: how to manage and control your accounts payable, accounts receivable, financial reports, balance sheets, income statements, payroll, job costing, collections, bonding, banking, month-end close-out, bank reconciliations, cash management, investments, and cash-flow projections.

A professional accounting manager knows what software your company needs, and can supervise its installation and fully maximize your return on investment. A professional accounting manager stays abreast of the latest tax and contract laws you may need to know, the best accounting methods, industry financial trends, and software upgrades, as well as attending training seminars and conferences and becoming a trusted partner in your business growth.

Install Financial Systems Now!

Trying to build a business without organized and systemized financial management tools and controls is like building a house with an empty toolbox and no plans. You can't do it. Make it a priority to install the best possible systems, technology, reporting methods, and tracking systems. This will allow you to make good decisions, keep your people accountable, help you keep your eyes on the bottom-line, and give you the time to focus on what makes the most money for your operation.

Entrepreneurial Excellence Business Tip:
Hire a professional accounting manager before you hire
your next employee or buy another piece of equipment.

Being in business is tough, especially if the market is in a downturn. Sometimes, for example, if you work on a commission basis in sales, things aren't always in your control. (You can't make people buy stuff they don't want or need!) It gets even harder when you don't know what your finances or direct costs are. You need financial systems and controls in order to build a strong business and hit your growth goals.

It's Hard to Go Broke with Good Financial Systems!

Sound financial management includes keeping track of several key success factors. Get your reports on time to stay on top of your company. Company owners without good accounting records and reports never know how they're doing, work too cheap, work too much, can't retire, and don't have investments.

Monthly financial reports you need:

- Direct job cost report for current accounts or projects
- Completed contracts for current fiscal year
- Income statement (profit and loss)
- Balance sheet (financial statement)
- Working capital
- Cash-flow projections
- Accounts receivable aging
- Accounts payables aging
- Cash report—all bank accounts

Weekly reports you need:

- Accounts receivable aging
- Current accounts payables
- Deposit log of payments received
- Cash needs
- Cash balances—all bank accounts
- Current payroll
- Line-of-credit status
- Discounts available

Let Go, But Keep Financial Control

Several years ago I learned the hard way that even good employees can go astray without sound financial controls in place. In most businesses, it's too tempting and very easy for trusted employees to "stick their hand in the cookie jar." I thought it would never happen in my company, but it did. I found the greed factor influenced some great employees to go over the ethical line and put a little extra in their pocket whenever possible. I trusted them too much, and didn't have proper checks and balances in place.

Financial troubles occur when there are no systems or controls, and only one person reviews every accounting operation. Some problem areas to watch out for include poor personnel or vacation records, credit card or reimbursable expenses not being reviewed, automatic payroll deposits not checked by the owner, company charge accounts not monitored, and materials being ordered for projects without approvals. Protect your money with financial controls.

Seven Financial Controls That Work!

1. Never issue company credit cards—let employees pay for items out of pocket and then get reimbursed.
2. Never issue company cell phones—give employees a monthly lump-sum amount ($75 to $150) to reimburse them for the use of their personal cell phones.
3. Have bank statements sent to the owner's home—this allows for review of checks and signatures.
4. Require the owner's or two managers' signatures and approvals on:

   - contracts that obligate the company
   - subcontracts, purchase orders, and change orders
   - payables and job costs
   - checks
   - credit card payments
   - automatic payroll deposits
   - reimbursable or expense accounts
   - overtime or vacation approvals
   - payroll preparation, approvals, and deposits

5. Keep perfect personnel, sick time, and vacation records—this is a must, with no exceptions for any employee, including friends, long-time employees, and even Uncle Joe.

6. Follow your employee manual to the letter—no exceptions for anyone, especially your long-time employees.
7. Trust your people, but follow your rules!

Today I still trust my people to do a great job, but I have installed these additional controls. A few simple checks and balances will eliminate most problems, disappointments, stress, and potential financial losses for your company. Don't wait until it's too late to implement financial safeguards and controls.

Get Rich or Die Trying!

You've heard the old saying: *"It's not how much you make; it's how much you keep."* The goal of business is not to stay in business. **The goal of business is to always make a profit.** An excellent business does more than keep money, it also uses it to create wealth.

> It's not how much you make, it's how much money your money makes!

Could a CEO of a major company survive without excellent financial systems and controls? No! To build a vibrant company, seek profitable accounts and customers, do quality work, and then collect all revenues earned. Cover the actual cost of your products, services, and doing work first. Next, pay your overhead. *Then* make a profit. As an entrepreneur, your biggest and most exciting decision is what to do with your profit—spend or invest.

A new startup company should be out of debt and making a return on their equity of at least 15 to 20 percent within the first five years. Within ten years, you should be making lots of profit and have several outside investments in place. After fifteen to twenty years in business, your company should be able to survive on its investment income alone if the economy slows and you can only break even. The greatest advice I give to young business owners is to buy your first investment property before your second truck. Real estate is a far better investment than a depreciating piece of yellow iron or equipment.

Financial Steps to Success

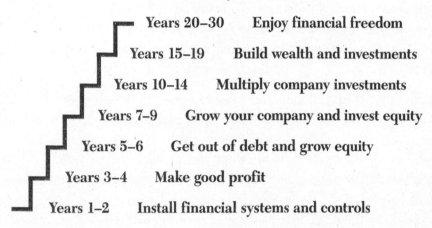

Years 20–30   Enjoy financial freedom

Years 15–19   Build wealth and investments

Years 10–14   Multiply company investments

Years 7–9   Grow your company and invest equity

Years 5–6   Get out of debt and grow equity

Years 3–4   Make good profit

Years 1–2   Install financial systems and controls

Who Is Your Spending Consultant?

Building a solid business is not easy. To maximize your return, follow the steps outlined above, plus get some outside professional help. You can't do it all yourself. You need a team of financial pros who can give you advice as your business grows. Your financial team should include a CPA, banker, insurance agent, attorney, and technology consultant. Get some professional advice and make installing financial systems and controls a priority and part of building an excellent business. You can't run your company in the dark. **Remember: the more you know, the more you can grow.**

Build Accurate Pricing and Cost Estimating Systems

As a contractor, this is my nightmare scenario: You negotiate an easy project with a great customer who trusts you, doesn't question your costs, and awards you the contract at your price. Then, seven months later, you discover that your cost estimator didn't put enough in the budget to cover all the work items required. Little things, like he forgot the roof! The time and energy spent building a trusted customer relationship has been wasted because of a poor cost estimate.

So, you ask your estimator, "What happened?" He blames it on the project manager, or the field superintendent, or the architect, or the engineer, or the weather, or bad plans, or his bad childhood! What do you do? You can't fire him. You need to bid on lots of work to keep the pipeline full. Plus, you don't have enough time to find and train another estimator. Now what?

Business is not easy! Building an excellent business is even tougher. Many successful companies were founded by entrepreneurs who are excellent at determining their costs and what to charge to stay busy and grow their business. **Doing the work or selling your products and services is important, but calculating accurate direct costs is necessary to make a profit.** To get a signed contract or order for your company's services or to sell products, you first find a sales lead or customer who needs what you offer. Then you must prove that your company is qualified to deliver. You determine the scope of what your customer requires, calculate what it will take to produce the finished product or service, secure vendor and supplier pricing, prepare your final cost estimate, mark it up, and then submit your proposal. Then you wait for the results of your efforts. The customer calls and asks you to revise your proposal to include more items. You let the customer know your new pricing structure. After the customer calls you again, you decide to cut your price more to get the order. Finally, you sign the contract and hope you'll make some money.

Accurate cost estimating and pricing systems are the foundation of overall business success. When you know your costs, you will manage better and make more profit. As your business grows, you have to delegate most of the cost estimating to others. To do this, you need to create and maintain accurate cost estimating and pricing systems and controls. As you develop these systems, remember that your goals are to replace yourself with systems that produce the same results every time. So, what is required to make this happen?

Know your direct costs.
Know your overhead costs.
Know your profit targets.

Know Your Direct Costs

The first goal of accurate cost estimating and pricing is to ensure that you know and can track direct product, service, labor, equipment, material, supplier, vendor, and/or subcontractor costs. With accurate direct costs, covering your overhead and hitting your profit targets becomes easier. Ask yourself these questions as you think about your pricing standards:

- *Do you know and track direct costs?*
- *Do you recap final costs versus the estimate?*
- *Do your timecards reflect the real employee costs per work item?*
- *Does your accounting system give timely direct cost reports?*
- *Do you have a cost history library?*
- *Do you feel confident in your costs?*
- *Is your production crew cost rate accurate?*
- *Are your equipment rates accurate?*
- *Is your overhead markup sufficient to recover your overhead?*
- *Is your profit markup enough to give you a proper return?*

What's Your Cost Estimator's #1 Priority?

When I speak at conferences and conventions, I get many responses to this question. They include:

- *Bid on lots of accounts or projects*
- *Get lots of work*
- *Be competitive*
- *Know what things cost*
- *Make a profit*

I Want Accuracy!

The top priority for my cost estimator should be to arrive at accurate direct costs. I don't want our final price to be *close* to what it might cost,

plus or minus 10 percent. Estimating accuracy is key to long-term business success. The only variable on any proposal or quotation should be
the profit markup. Excellent and experienced cost estimators know what
things cost. In my opinion, your cost estimating goal must be to prepare
price estimates within 1 or 2 percent of the final actual cost. Good estimators continually compare their current pricing to past results to see how
accurate they were. Then they make adjustments accordingly for their next
proposals. They are in constant contact with production, suppliers, vendors, and subcontractors to determine how they arrive at estimated costs.

Accurate Pricing and Estimating Rules

1. Every cost estimate covers your final direct costs. Your cost estimating
and pricing goal is to calculate the accurate final cost of your service or
product. Estimates should not include any "fat" or "fudge factor" or "slop"
to cover unknowns. A perfect estimate will equal your final actual cost
within a few percentage points.

2. Your estimate is the total cost. Your cost estimator's job is to arrive at
the total cost. To arrive at accurate costs, cost estimators are responsible
for knowing what things cost. They must update their cost history library
on an ongoing basis.

3. Your bid is the total sales or contract amount. A bid is the sum of
accurate estimated direct costs plus your overhead markup plus your profit
markup to hit your overall company goals. Can you cut your direct costs or
indirect overhead costs when pricing products or services? No—both are
fixed amounts. The only pricing variable is profit. Profit is the reward for
taking a business risk and should be adjusted based on risk and the return
you want on each sale, account, project, service, or product.

What is the most risky thing you do? For most companies, employee labor
is the hardest to control and where most cost overruns occur. Think of
your profit markup as a risk factor to cover the variables of producing your
product or service.

4. Contracts are opportunities! When you are awarded a contract or
receive an order to perform services or provide products, what do you

have? An opportunity to get paid for direct costs to cover your labor, equipment, material, vendors, and subcontractors. Then you have an additional opportunity to make some money—after you recover your overhead. Your overhead is a set amount determined by your fixed cost of doing business.

$ales Is the Answer to Your Profit Problem

1. Can you make money on every sale, yet still lose money?
2. When do you make a profit?
3. What are your options if your:
   - *overhead increases?*
   - *volume decreases?*
   - *markup decreases?*
   - *direct costs increase?*

Many times I have listened to business owners lament that they can't get enough markup to make a net profit. Or they complain that they have to price their services and products too cheap, and then they come in costing more than they estimated. The problem is simple. Basic business math must be understood.

Sales

- Direct Cost

- Overhead

= Net Profit

You can cover your direct costs on every sale, and still not have enough leftover to recover your overhead or make a profit. This usually happens to owners who don't understand business fundamentals. You don't make a profit until all of your annual direct costs are paid for *and* you pay back all of your overhead costs for the year. Most companies don't cover their overhead costs until October or November and don't make a profit until December. Just because you have money in the bank doesn't mean your business is profitable.

When you increase overhead by renting a bigger office or shop, or hiring a new salesperson, manager, or bookkeeper, your choices are simple: *raise markup or increase sales volume*. If your volume or markup decreases in a softening market, your only choices are to cut overhead or increase sales. When your direct costs increase you're in trouble, because your only choice is more sales. Most owners mistakenly focus on cutting costs instead of increasing revenue when things go bad.

Is Your Bid a Mystery?

Cost overruns occur when business owners use standard pricing models or unit prices to price their services, products, or work. Art dealers charge for framing a picture by the square foot. Cleaners charge the same price for every men's white dress shirt they launder. Stores charge the same price per candy bar, regardless of their order size. Lawyers and accountants generally charge every client the same hourly rate regardless of the business, transaction, or complexity. Concrete sidewalk contractors charge by the square foot of sidewalk, regardless of the job size or difficulty. Over time, these simple unit prices become their standards. And as prices rise for labor, materials, or equipment, business owners don't make proper adjustments, and instead start guessing at the real costs. I call this the "mystery method" of cost estimating.

At a fencing contractors association meeting I asked 100 contractors how much a six-foot chain-link fence costs. Everyone answered the same: $11 per lineal foot installed. I then asked if it mattered how big the job was, how difficult the job was, if the access was easy, or if the foundations were to be poured in rock, dirt, or into an existing asphalt parking lot. They didn't know how to calculate the different conditions to vary their bids accurately. They didn't keep a library of their costs that would allow them to accurately calculate different direct costs for changing conditions, customers, and quantities.

A good accounting software package tracks labor time by the type of work or service performed and then gives tracking reports on the exact costs expended on each part of the work produced. Make it your priority to acquire an excellent job cost accounting software package that will help build your company.

Want to Make Lots of Money?

Make your cost estimate more than a "guesstimate." Make each estimate an exact prediction of what it will take to produce every product, perform every service, or sell every product you offer. Install accurate financial systems, accurate estimating and pricing systems, and cost controls. And then watch your bottom-line results improve significantly.

Step 3: Build Financial, Pricing, and Profit Systems!

Business-Builder Action Plans

1. Decide if you are a money-maker or a money-saver.
2. Decide what you have to do to become profit-driven.
3. Seek opportunities to maximize your bottom-line.
4. Know and track your numbers. (Worksheet #14)
5. Set specific, fixed annual financial targets.
6. Track your contracts, accounts receivables, liabilities, and cash.
7. Give yourself a raise.
8. Hire a financial professional.
9. Install financial systems and software.
10. Set financial controls.
11. Install accurate pricing systems.
12. When in doubt, sell more!

To download the Business-Builder Worksheets, visit:
GetYourBusinessToWork.com/book

Build Operational Systems!

Would you go to Starbucks if the lattes weren't consistent every time, from store to store? Every company must do several things perfectly and consistently in order to be successful. If these important things aren't adhered to in a systematic and standardized way, the customer will stop doing business with the company. Your company can't grow if you do things in a disorganized and chaotic manner. With all the different pressures of building a profitable company, **it's often tempting to do things out of sequence or by the seat of your pants.**

Have you ever hired a manager, salesperson, or employee too quickly, without proper screening or reference checks, because you were too busy and needed to fill an empty slot to get your work completed? Then, several weeks later, because you didn't have enough time to properly supervise or train him, you discover he's not doing the job the way you want it done. Busy, out-of-control business owners make hasty decisions because they don't take time to stop, plan, think, and do what it takes to build an organized and systemized company.

Is your company operating at full capacity, but missing a few parts and held together with duct tape?

Do you make hasty customer, purchasing, or employee decisions because you don't have enough time to research all the options and then put the right pieces together? Do you get stuck using the same suppliers, vendors, and subcontractors because you don't have enough time to find new or better ones? Do you personally order and schedule all employees and material deliveries because you don't have a system in place to allow your supervisor or office manager to do it for you? Are you too busy to take your best customers to lunch on a regular basis so you can create quality relationships with them? Do you end up going from job to job making sure your employees or crews are doing things the way you want them done? Do you have to make every major and minor decision for your people? When is the last time your project manager held a meeting without you leading it? Are you too busy working to fully understand your actual costs, company financials, or profit targets? When did you last take time to sit down with each of your employees and thank them for a job well done? Do you take time to track, update, and review your department, project, or company goals with your key people? Do you keep trying and trying to build a better company but can't seem to make it happen?

You know what you need to do. Why aren't you doing it?

Most stressed-out business owners want to make changes, but most never figure out how to let go of the reins. Earl owns a wholesale printing company. After he saw me speak at a national convention, he signed up for one of my two-day business owner Profit-Builder Circle academies. I got to know him well. His business had the potential to grow and make a lot more money than it was making at its current sales level. But he was stuck at his level of control.

His goal after the workshop was to install twenty operational systems to free himself up to focus on generating more business. A year later I e-mailed him to get an update on his progress. He had created the systems, but still didn't have enough time to go out and call on any new customers. Why? He was still spending all his time checking in on his managers and employees. He didn't trust them to do as good a job as he wanted. He told me he had great people, but they still made too many mistakes, were often inefficient, too slow, wasteful with materials, didn't care enough about the customers, and didn't work as hard as he did. So he had to keep helping them do their jobs. Earl had created systems to follow, but wouldn't allow his people to do their jobs without his constant interference and control. He was now at an even higher level of frustration. Sound like a familiar story to you?

After conducting a survey of Earl's employees, they informed me they wished he would let them do their jobs, stop worrying about all the little details, get out of the office, and go out and get some more work.

In my case, when I finally realized I couldn't be at every construction job site and watch everything for everybody, I had a choice: keep doing business in an out-of-control manner, or stop, decide to replace myself with operational systems, and allow my employees and managers to do their jobs. Written systems, guidelines, and checklists allowed me to show people what was expected, trust them to do the job properly, let go, and then work on getting our company to grow. The systems took me away from constant, full-time supervision, micromanaging, and continuously giving directions, which freed me to focus on important things like customers, profitability, and leading my company.

Earl had to make the same decision most business owners face at some point in their company growth. **Let go or you won't grow!** He started by promoting three managers to department heads. He then had to delegate the system management and work processes. This was hard for him, and it took him several months to finally make it happen. He didn't want to let go of setting prices, buying any materials over $500, hiring and firing, charging customers more than the original quote, or giving out performance bonuses to employees without checking with him first. He would tell his managers: **"You are hereby 100 percent accountable to make every major decision. Just check with me first!"**

This is not leadership. This management style is controlling, distrustful, operating out of fear, and won't work if you want to grow your company.

Nothing happens without your involvement when you don't have good systems in place and you don't allow your people to do a good job without you always reminding them or telling them what to do.

> **What happens or doesn't happen when you do it all yourself? NOTHING!**

The more YOU do, the less your people do.

When you make all the decisions and constantly tell your employees how you want things done, they won't grow. This toxic behavior stops people from wanting to contribute more and become the best they can be. When you finally discover that **the problem with your people is not them, but you**, you'll realize that good people alone won't solve your problems. Six different excellent and experienced people will still do things six different ways. This is not the solution to your company's growth challenges. Earl had to look at which decisions he really wanted to be involved with. In the end he decided the only decisions he wanted to approve were things that affected customer relationships and firing employees. He finally let go, trusted his management team to work together to make good everyday decisions, and figured that with his leadership, he could keep the company moving toward positive growth targets and profitability.

Start by making a list of the top ten things in each area of your business that you absolutely must do perfectly for your company to be successful. For example, if you are a concrete subcontractor, you'd better have a system in place to ensure that concrete slabs are installed properly and do not randomly crack. If you own a printing business, you'd better have a system in place to ensure that the customer approves the proof, design, layout, copy, color, and paper before you print their order. When pricing a new product or service, you'd better have systems in place that give you accurate costs to use to calculate your proposal price. If you want to make a profit, you must have financial systems in place to track and collect money owed, forecast your cash needs, and track your overhead and profit goals.

Let's talk about your company's operational systems in more depth. As you walk from office to office asking your key managers and supervisors how things are going, their responses probably include:

"Everything's O.K."

"Ninety-nine percent complete; just a few little things left."

"I think we'll finish on time."

"I'm getting all the customer approval signatures tomorrow."

"The paperwork is almost done."

"We're coming in close to budget."

"Only a few issues left to resolve."

"No problems I can't handle."

But are things really going as well as you are told? A few days later, you get a call from an angry customer screaming that his order is three weeks late. Another is upset she is not getting the quality and service she contracted for. A third demands you drop everything and fix his problem *now*. Your office manager tells you some account managers are not doing their required paperwork on time, and several orders did not get checked before they were assembled and shipped. An irate supplier calls threatening to cancel the next shipment unless they get paid for the previous three shipments which were delivered over two months ago . . .

And then it gets even worse. Your accounts receivable aging report does not look good: many accounts are several weeks overdue. Four customers still owe you money on projects completed over three months ago. There are several outstanding items left to complete on four projects from over a year ago. You have six outstanding invoices customers refuse to pay. The month-end cost report shows the anticipated final profit on five projects has slipped again without notice.

No problems?!?

These issues are symptomatic of companies run by owners who haven't taken the time to install and maintain proactive operational systems. They struggle and fail as they let managers and employees continually tell them what they want to hear—instead of the truth. This avoids conflict until it's too late to overlook. Typical management problems are encountered when companies don't have standardized systems in place to guarantee that everyone does business the same way with a sure-fire follow-up procedure to make sure the systems were actually followed. You want consistent performance and results. You want everyone to do business in a similar manner, on-time, with consistent standards. You don't want to be constantly reminding, checking, and confronting to make sure everything is performed exactly the way you want it done. You don't want those irate customer phone calls. You want your managers to be accountable and keep you informed of the real situation on every account, project, product, service, order, customer, delivery, or contract.

Even if you have great managers, they will all do things differently unless you have written systems in place for everyone to follow. Six good managers, salespeople, or employees will do things six different ways—late, halfway, organized, unorganized, or not at all. This creates chaos, disorganization, stress, and loss of profits. Your customers, suppliers, vendors, and subcontractors can't deal with a company that doesn't have consistent business standards and systems in place or followed. Could you imagine doing business with a bank that let each loan officer lend based on their own personal standards? Or a printing business where each designer could decide if and when customers were required to sign off on a proof before it went to print? Would Starbucks be successful if each barista was allowed to decide how many scoops of coffee went into every pot? None of them would work.

Typical recurring problems, like those described above, are a result of company owners not requiring everyone to follow the company operational systems. Most companies have general rules to follow, but don't have them written down. And if they are written down, they are not enforced or reviewed for compliance on a regular basis. Plus employees are not forced or trained to follow company standards of customer service, production, quality, or installation methods. The owner tries to keep managers and employees herded like cats to follow the company rules and systems. But busy owners, over time, let their people slip from following company procedures, if they even have them. It's hard to keep people accountable to systems that aren't clearly understood, written, reviewed, trained, tracked, followed, adhered to, and made mandatory.

Super-efficient, super-fast, and super-productive companies are focused on more than getting their work done. They focus on being super-organized and have a super-systemized, proactive approach to management. This allows them to:

- *Produce consistent results*
- *Start and finish projects fast*
- *Be on time*
- *Stay on budget*
- *Meet their commitments*
- *Keep customers happy*
- *Create a great place to work*
- *Identify problems early*
- *Train and improve people*
- *Maximize and allocate resources*
- *Make above-average profits*
- *Grow without additional problems*

What Are Proactive Operational Systems?

Proactive operational systems are repeatable, standardized, written organizational methods, procedures, and guidelines. Their purpose is to achieve company goals and optimize time, energy, money, people, equipment, and materials within a specific deadline.

Management performs several different types of activities, such as planning, assessing risk, estimating resources, organizing work, assigning tasks, directing activities, monitoring, tracking, reporting progress, and analyzing results. Proactive operational systems control all business activities and deliver the desired and targeted results on time and on budget, in a super-efficient, super-fast, super-productive, and super-organized manner.

Good People or Good Systems?

As a contractor, I make it a priority to visit our construction job sites on a regular basis. Before we had organized field operational systems in place, every time I went to the job site, lots of things were going wrong. We were overly reliant on our people to get our jobs built on time with the quality expected by our customers and contracts. It took experienced field supervisors and foremen to ensure that every project detail was perfect. But problems continued to occur as every project manager, supervisor, foreman, and crew leader did things the best way he or she knew how. Sometimes that was the way I wanted it done, but usually not.

This reliance on good people instead of good company procedures and systems caused lots of field problems, unpredictable quality, late projects, unhappy customers, and lost profits. Since I didn't have enough time in the day to inspect everyone's work, our project teams created lots of callbacks, long lists of items to fix, and ongoing warranty issues. This inconsistency in our work quality and service became overwhelming, and it reduced our ability to grow our business.

No systems = no controls = no customers
= no money!!

Most likely, your overall company goal is to make every project, product, and service a success for you and your customers. You pride yourself on quality workmanship and on-time completion at a fair price by providing full value and full service. This is difficult to deliver without good systems in place, unless you are everywhere, making sure everything is done correctly. This gets out of control as your company grows from one to five, from fifteen to twenty-five people or more. Think of the worst project, account, service, or customer you've been involved with. What went wrong?

Regardless of what problems or challenges you've faced, **most likely the real problem was a lack of written company operational systems.** Problems can be solved by making it your overall company priority to get everyone on the same page, doing things the same way. You currently try to let your people do their best, but you don't have a process in place to show them what you want, train them to do it properly, follow up, and make them accountable. When you don't have company standards and systems, you rely on each person to do things the way he or she thinks is best. This doesn't ensure consistent performance and bottom-line results.

Do it different or do it right!

It's hard to make people responsible when they don't have a clear picture of what you want. What systems do you have in place to ensure that everyone does things per company guidelines and standards? If you rely on word of mouth or your constant inspection, you'll never build an excellent company. Great people who don't follow company standards create problems and chaos. How would you like to get your bank statement sent out differently every month, or to have your favorite restaurant make your favorite meal too spicy, too bland, or too salty, depending who cooked it that night?

Without systems in place, you are at the mercy of your people, managers, employees, and supervisors to do a good job. Documented written systems allow you to reduce problems and deliver to your customer every time. Remember the old saying "Measure twice, cut once"? This is an example of a simple system and a proven standard that works. The reason your projects don't finish on time is because you haven't made scheduling, meeting, and communication standards a priority in your company. To build an excellent company, create, draft, and implement operational systems to minimize problems and maximize profits!

Be Proactive to Make More Profit!

You can get your business to work without your constant attention by creating, installing, and using operational systems. The results you get are a direct result of your priorities and how you run and manage your company. **To make more money and have more fun with less stress, get organized!** Install systems to produce consistent results and get everyone in your company doing business the same way.

A key factor in owning and managing an organized and systemized company is to select the systems that will ensure the success of your operations. **To create proactive project management systems, start by selecting the top ten systems that, if implemented and followed, will guarantee successful results 90 percent of the time.** Then focus on creating and maintaining these systems. It will be your job to monitor your systems and force your team to adhere to them without exception. Here is list of some management systems you may want to start with. Select the top ten you feel will eliminate the most problems, make you the most money, produce consistent results, and ensure excellence.

____ Ongoing safety program	____ Ongoing employee training
____ Material ordering checklist	____ Inventory control system
____ Proposal checklist	____ Pre-delivery checklist
____ Purchase order checklist	____ Required approvals list
____ Insurance requirements	____ Opening and closing procedures
____ Project schedule updates	____ Project startup checklist
____ Contract scope standards	____ Customer service standards
____ Production checklist	____ Job cost reporting and review

____ Payment and invoicing   ____ Paperwork
     procedures

____ Documentation checklist   ____ Administration procedures

____ Project management checklist ____ Communication standards

Systems You Must Do—Or Die!

At Hedley Construction, we selected, installed, and continue to monitor up to fifteen must-do management systems. One of our systems is the mandatory one-hour monthly project management meeting. This system ensures that the project team meets every month to review and monitor the progress of every project in process. The attendees include the entire project team: project manager, engineer, superintendent, foreman, contract administrator, and bookkeeper. In this valuable meeting, we follow the same agenda every month. We review the progress of each project under contract. We review and check that each project system is being followed and whether the project is on track and meeting its goals. We verify:

Project target tracking	Contract checklist
Executed contract	Procurement log
Updated schedule	Progress photos
Project change log	Approvals required log
Accounts receivable	Accounts payable
Job cost update	Budget variance report

Must Do Operational Systems

1. Install One System Every Two Weeks

Business is always changing and continually needs improvement as you grow, change your product mix, improve your service, find new projects, seek new customers, and hire more people to do the work. If you continue to do business the same way, you won't improve or get better. Look at professional sports. Teams are always coming up with new plays, trying new things, and constantly working on new ways to beat their competition. As a business owner or manager, you must also constantly improve and refine the way your company does things. My ongoing goal is to install one new system every two weeks. Our goal is twenty-five new or improved "plays" every year. As you create and improve your Must-Do playbook, start with the things you want done perfectly to guarantee the success of your company. Your goal is to create a winning playbook you can use as a training tool and guide how you want things done. Remember, *if it's not a written playbook*, everything is still in your head, you will be the only one calling the plays, and *your company will continue to be stuck* at the level of your ability to control everything.

2. Manage the Systems

A business that works is controlled, systemized, and organized. The business is run by the systems—not the owner. The owner manages the systems—*instead of doing the work*. The systemized company produces the same consistent results every time. This guarantees repeat loyal customers, a safe working environment, quality workmanship, on-time deliveries, empowered and accountable employees, and an above-average profit margin. With systems in place, your job changes from micromanaging and controlling every move for every employee to making sure the company systems are followed to deliver perfect results.

A simple follow-up procedure for every Must-Do company or project system allows you to make sure each system was adhered to. For example, a printing company must have a pre-print checklist system to ensure that everything is approved and ready for a perfect print job. Before printing an order, the print foreman will make sure all of items on the checklist are checked off. He initials every item and signs the form as complete. Then he puts it with the order file. Your job is to make sure he followed the Must-Do system by looking at the completed file on an ongoing basis. If it's left for the foreman to decide if and when the checklist is completed, it won't happen on every order. The print shop owner then won't have to supervise the foreman or watch the actual printing job in progress to see if he followed the company system. The system will force him to do it the company way.

3. Set and Track Targets

Every employee on your project team needs to know what they're responsible for and when they're successful. Playing basketball without a basket or scoreboard would not be very exciting. Working for a company without a scorecard or targets to hit would not be very exciting either. People need regular weekly feedback and information about their progress and achievement. This allows them to stay on track and make adjustments to improve and keep on course. What measurable targets can your employees use to hit the goals for their work? What do you want to track? What will keep people focused on the results you expect? Everyone needs three or four things to strive for every week, which they can measure. For example, a warehouse shipping team can track accurate orders shipped, the number of on-time deliveries, and the total number of orders handled. Each of these areas can be quantified and measured every week. Your job is to make sure the team members get the proper input and feedback to set their targets and track their results.

4. Manage Your Money

As I said in Chapter 3, many business owners aren't focused on their bottom-line. They're focused on getting work done, hoping they make enough money to pay the bills and have a little left over to pay for their lifestyle or buy a new boat. They think of accounting as a necessary evil instead of a valuable part of their success. **Why are you in business, to do quality work or make a profit?** How can you make a profit without attention to financial details? I didn't say write the checks, I said manage the money and focus on hitting your financial goals. The big financial numbers you must know, watch, control, and manage include:

- Sales volume
- Direct or job costs
- Fixed overhead expenses
- Company gross profit
- Company net profit
- Monthly cash-flow
- Weekly cash balances
- Accounts payable and receivable aging

Most accounting managers and employees are focused on paying the bills and aren't worried about making money. **Unless *you* are focused on making money**, know what it takes to make a profit, and have systems in place to track and monitor your progress, **it won't happen**. Know your numbers, manage your financial systems, and watch your bank account grow.

5. Make People a Priority

I am sick and tired of hearing people say that they can't find any good trained help. Duh! There aren't any good trained professionals sitting in front of your office waiting for you! Good trained help is a result of you making people a priority, building a great place to work, and having systems in place to make sure your people are recognized, motivated, and on track to meeting their goals. A great place to work has an ongoing training program where employees are involved in at least forty hours of training every year. There are incentives in place for employees to recruit others to your company and encourage their friends to apply for jobs. There are reasons people want to work for your company. You have systems in place for your people to be inspired, recognized, and praised on a regular basis. Your systems empower people to make decisions, become accountable and responsible. Cutting-edge ideas, methods, and technology must be used and encouraged. The best companies are organized and systemized, and the boss is a coach instead of a control freak who screams and barks orders.

Proven People Systems

Leaders who make people a priority do four simple things.

1. Provide clear expectations. These are written, measurable systems, goals, and targets for employees to follow. Written systems that are trained, monitored, and tracked allow people to understand exactly what is expected of them on an ongoing basis.	*3. Show employees you care about them.* To make people a priority, keep a chart for every employee and make sure you meet with them two to four times a year. Ask them what they hope for in their future, what interests them about their job, how you can help them reach their goals, and take an interest in their family and personal life.
2. Recognize and praise employees. People systems ensure that every employee gets thanked, recognized, and praised every week by their supervisor. Use a tracking system to make sure it happens. Use words like "Thank you for . . ." and "I appreciate how you . . ." when commenting on what people have done or accomplished.	*4. Take time to explain the big picture.* Have a standard way of keeping everyone informed about how the company is doing and how it affects the future for employees. People want to know what's happening: sales, customers, profit, changes, opportunities, growth, or expansion. If you don't hold regular company meetings, your people remain in the dark and stay worried about their future.

6. Delegate

What is holding your company back from profitable growth? *Is it YOU?* When you delegate to others, they become more valuable and responsible. This allows you to concentrate on things that make a big difference in your future. Every day, go through your in-basket and to-do list and delegate at least one thing to every key manager or employee. This habit will become one of the best things you ever do.

7. Mandatory Meetings

Unsuccessful people are usually too busy to hold meetings. Meetings are a simple way to manage systems, leverage yourself, and communicate expectations to your employees, managers, subcontractors, vendors, and suppliers. The most important meetings for me are:

- ### Daily Team Huddle-Up Meeting

  Can you imagine a football team winning games without calling plays before every down? Before every play in football, the team huddles up to discuss what they're going to do next, making sure everyone knows their role and what they're expected to do. In your company, in your production or field crews, a similar huddle is a must if you want your teams to be winners. This will improve your bottom-line as daily activities become better coordinated and focused on what end results are expected by team captains or foremen. Like a football huddle, this should be a short meeting where everyone stands in a circle and talks about the upcoming daily activities, targets, goals, conflicts, confusions, schedule, material, equipment, tools, and deadlines.

- ### Monday Morning Quarterback Meeting

  Every week on winning football teams, coaches review their team's accomplishments, progress, needs, challenges, and areas for improvement; and then they decide what they need to do over the next week to achieve their goals. On Monday morning, they meet with their entire team, review the game plan for the week, and discuss what needs to be done to make it happen. Every production crew, management team, division, or department needs a similar program to get everyone focused on their game plan for the upcoming week. Meet on Monday mornings in a convenient place where everyone can get involved and contribute. Use visual charts to explain the goals and plays like football coaches. Discuss key success factors, such as production targets, finances, customer satisfaction, quality requirements, scheduling milestones, revenue, or expenses. Also use this meeting for training and safety.

- **Project or New Account Startup Meeting**

  Before a football game begins, the coaches have spent many hours together mapping out their game plan. They have discussed every possibility for success and failure. Then they decide the best way to execute their plan. In order to keep projects on track, the same amount of advanced planning is required by the project management team. The culmination of this project pre-planning is the presentation of the game plan to the project players, employees, vendors, subcontractors, and suppliers. This meeting will force your project managers, supervisors, and foremen to get together in advance and create a project plan.

- **Weekly Project Field Coordination Meeting**

  This one meeting can improve your overall completion and schedules by 25 percent or more. By getting every team player together on a regular basis, they become aware of the urgency of the situation. You have heard the statement "Out of sight, out of mind." This is reality. Vendors who get phone calls from your managers or supervisors to discuss upcoming orders or needs only hear the pleas. But once they see the project moving forward, they become aware of the schedule and then make it their priority as well. This is a mandatory meeting, no exceptions. Your employees won't want to hold this meeting because they don't want to push their people too hard or stand up in front of a crowd and take charge.

But force them to hold these meetings and the results will be incredible.

- ## Monthly Project Management Meeting

  I call this the "accountability" meeting, where each project, division, or department team meets monthly and shows their boss how well they're doing on their jobs or areas of responsibility. In these one-hour meetings, review every project's accomplishments, budgets, goals, schedules, financials, and progress. This meeting will hold people accountable for following the company systems, managing their projects properly, doing their job as expected, and hitting their targets.

- ## Company Monthly Management Meeting

  This is an overall company strategy session to discuss the direction of your company, what's working, and what needs improvement. The agenda can include any major decision, new services, products, programs, finances, sales, customers, service, personnel, or any other subject requiring discussion or consensus. Part of the discussions should include open debate and review of all the options available to solve your company's future choices. The agenda should include monitoring and review of overall company strategy, progress on company goals, old and new business, and action plans.

- ## Company-Wide Town Hall Meeting

  One of the most important things employees need in order to stay motivated is information about the direction and future of their company. On a regular basis, each person needs to know about the "big picture" and where the company is going. By holding regular company-wide town hall meetings, you can inform everyone of what's happening at your company. In this meeting, tell the truth about the company's future, direction, decisions, new policies, targets, finances, backlog, equipment, systems, customers, and issues. Review past accomplishments and failures. Explain where or what improvements are needed. Discuss future goals and how your company hopes to hit them. Then ask for suggestions, questions, input, and ideas. As part of this meeting, provide some training on new systems or procedures from the office and field operations. Also use this opportunity to recognize people who have done a great job, and present awards for special accomplishments.

- ## Management Planning Retreat

At the end of every football season, the coaches and management team get together for a few days to look at how well they did, their current situation, and what it will take to improve over the next year. In your company, an annual meeting is an important time for company management to decide on the overall direction, strategic issues, changes, adjustments, people, customers, priorities, and approaches necessary to achieve desired results. Hold this meeting at an off-site location so that each attendee will stay focused on the agenda. Start with a review of the company's past performance. Then look at where the company is today. And then decide where you want to go and what actions will be required to achieve your goals. A realistic discussion of the economy and opportunities available is required to determine what challenges are facing your company. A comprehensive review of your people and management team should be done, including decisions about future needs and changes. A thorough discussion of all company goals and targets for the upcoming years should be part of this meeting as well.

Run your company like a winning football team. Each of these meetings works! But they may not all be right for your company. The most important thing is to hold regular meetings. Start with one or two of these meetings to see how effective they are for your company. Then try another one in an area where you need the most work. But remember, when you never hold meetings, you are carrying the entire company on your shoulders and not getting the full support of your team.

8. Make Production a Priority

Most hourly employees think only a few hours ahead. In order to improve production results, install simple productivity systems to help your managers, supervisors, and foremen look ahead and think about what's required to keep production efficient, fast, and running like a machine. Require four-week look-ahead schedules to be prepared weekly. This forces each team leader to draft his or her schedule of activities needed to occur in the next four weeks. Provide blank charts for team leaders to draft what's needed, upcoming milestones, and requirements.

To improve quality and safety, require every supervisor to take a few minutes every Wednesday to look for potential safety issues and quality improvement areas, then fill out a pre-printed form describing the work or problem observed, along with their recommendations to remedy the situation, the responsible party, and when the problem area must be fixed. This forces project team leaders to look for and anticipate problems before they occur. It also notifies people and companies to fix problems now and not wait until the final product is produced and it is too late to fix them.

You wouldn't start a construction project without a detailed set of working drawings or plans to build from. Management is no different. **There are certain steps every project must follow that guarantee on-time and on-budget completion and success.** These steps must be identified and perfected as part of your management system. These systems can include meetings, procurement procedures, order processing standards, inventory control, or checklists to ensure every activity is completed.

The objective is more than to keep the work flow moving. It is to hit the goals and project milestones. Written and monitored systems will make this happen. You must break down the work flow into small, incremental steps that will ensure that the end results are accomplished. By creating and following a plan, the manager can assign tasks and hold people accountable.

The next step is to implement the process or work flow. Ongoing organizational systems will keep your employees headed toward the desired end result. Each team member must know what is expected and what systems must be followed before starting work. By establishing clear measurements and procedures for implementation, team members can get started on track and can be monitored on an ongoing basis as to their progress. Consider which systems will guarantee the results you want.

Constant monitoring becomes easy for the owner and upper management when systems are in place and being followed. When production systems are installed and used effectively, monthly evaluation meetings become a simple matter of checking what has been done properly and what needs attention. When systems are used, problems become easy to identify, hard to overlook or hide, and can be addressed before it's too late.

Project Startup Checklist

____ Review bid, estimate, and proposal

____ Set project goals and objectives

____ Complete project administration checklist

____ Verify billing and payment procedures

____ Prepare schedule

____ Assess special tools and equipment needed

____ Determine loading and unloading needs

____ Read complete contracts and documents

____ Set up master budget

____ Verify insurance requirements

____ Analyze cash-flow needs

____ Verify deadlines and long lead items

____ Create meeting schedules

____ Figure out project close-out requirements

9. Know Your Costs

Profit starts with your estimate. Mandatory Must-Do systems need to include accurate time cards to obtain accurate direct or job costs. A fully integrated job cost and accounting system must be installed and maintained to grow your profitable business. This will allow you to keep an accurate cost history for each type of task or project you perform, resulting in accurate estimates.

10. Constant Customer Contact

Want to make a lot of money? Go see your top ten to twenty customers every two to three months. Take them to lunch or dinner, to a ball game or an industry event. Get to know them. Find out what makes them tick. See what it takes to make them want to use your company. Money is made by creating relationships with your top customers. If you don't install systems to build customer relationships, your only method to sell more services or products or get more work is to price low and hope customers will come in the door or call you when they need what you offer.

** 11. Bonus Must-Do!—Seek Wealth-Building Opportunities

When I speak at conventions, people often ask me for my best business tip. My advice is to buy your building before your next truck or piece of equipment. **Wealthy company owners own real estate.** Poor owners own debt, fixtures, and equipment. The choice is yours!

By replacing yourself with operational production systems, you'll have time to buy your own building, seek better customers, look for profitable accounts, find better people, and seek strategic business opportunities. When you work too hard and make all the everyday decisions, you'll never have time to get better, and you'll peak at the level of what you control. It's your choice:

Die trying to do it all yourself
or
replace yourself with
written operational systems!

Install Training Systems That Work

I played water polo in high school and college. After summer vacation, our two-week training camp would start in early September. It was tough. Twice a day for two hours per session, we would swim laps, pass the ball, practice our skills, shoot goals, lift weights, and work on our offensive and defensive techniques. When I first arrived at camp, my ball handling was clumsy and my swimming was weak. But as I trained I got better, and I actually improved over my level achieved the previous season.

After our skills returned to a competent level, the coach would show us new ways to improve. We practiced new skills until they became easy. The coach would constantly watch us practice, giving us feedback on our progress. Often he would get into the water to show us how to do the moves better. Throughout the season, he would teach us strategies to make us better players and a better team. By the end of every season, we had learned lots of new skills and tricks to use during the games to help us outwit and outscore the competition. The coach always built winning teams with near-perfect records using this relentless pursuit of perfection.

Is Your Company Getting Rusty?

Treat your business exactly like competitive sports. Without ongoing training and practice, people get rusty, out of shape, and don't improve at what they do. They get used to doing the same old things the same old way at the same level, and they become complacent. Training helps people grow and expand their ability to work at a faster pace with more proficiency and excellence. Every season I would swim faster than the previous year, and my 100-yard freestyle time would improve at least 5 percent. Your people can get faster and better too with an ongoing training program.

Should You Invest in Training?

Do you wish your employees were as good as you? Do they often struggle and fail to do things the way you want them done? Are your people as efficient as they should be? Do your employees sit and wait for their boss to make simple decisions for them? Or do your people constantly improve and try new and better ways to do things? Do your people like to make changes and master new tasks?

It's human nature to keep doing things the same old way. For example, I bet you drive to work the same way every day! **Most people don't try new ideas** on their own because they are afraid of making a mistake and incurring their boss's wrath, and because the way they're doing it works. What you want to do is make it work *better*! The good news is that most people *want* to do better, learn new things, and grow. Training is the best method to encourage and make your people feel comfortable about changing and improving their game.

Are You Keeping Up with Your Competition?

When I surveyed thousands of business owners, over 98 percent said their people would do a better job if they provided more training. But this awareness doesn't lead to action! The following survey results show how much training per year per employee companies actually perform.

Small Business Production Employee Training Per Year

51%	0–8 hours
20%	9–16 hours
19%	17–40 hours
10%	over 40 hours

Small Business Management Employee Training Per Year

35%	0–8 hours
25%	9–16 hours
20%	17–40 hours
20%	over 40 hours

<table>
<tr><td colspan="2">Fortune 500 Company Training Per Employee Per Year</td></tr>
<tr><td>80%</td><td>over 40 hours</td></tr>
</table>

Some 51 percent of small businesses don't make training a priority and only provide up to eight hours of training per employee per year. Only 10 percent of these companies invest forty hours of training per year in their production employees. Surprisingly, 35 percent of companies offer less than eight hours of training for management personnel per year. And only 20 percent train their managers for forty hours or more. Contrast this with the more than 80 percent of all Fortune 500 companies which average more than forty hours of training per year per employee!

Most small companies surveyed train their management more than their rank-and-file workers. This doesn't make sense if you're concerned about quality, service, and productivity—all of that happens at the customer service end.

Are You Too Busy to Train?

You live the vicious cycle: as companies grow, the owner takes on more work than she can handle alone. So she hires some help to assist her. Then, as her team grows and her daily job pressures mount, she has difficulty finding good help to delegate responsibility to. She knows she should train her people, but she doesn't have time. She is too busy to train and too busy to be at all places all the time. What should she do?

Most owners continue to try and make all the decisions themselves and control everything. This never works, as the employees are held back and not allowed to grow. This causes productivity to decrease and production costs to increase. And then good employees leave for better opportunities.

No Training Is Draining!

Most small companies don't have formal training programs. **In today's high-tech, high-speed business environment, people need to learn and improve 50 percent every four years just to stay even.** Maybe your firm is too busy to train because you expect people to learn in a vacuum, or by the trial-and-error method, or from their previous boss at their last company.

People want to make meaningful contributions on the job. They want to be recognized for their efforts. They need training to keep up, and additional training to excel. If they don't get the training and tools they need, they won't accept responsibility for the quality and productivity of the work they do and won't grow into productive team players.

The 2 Percent Investment

To improve productivity and stay ahead of the competition, **your ongoing company training program must provide a minimum of forty hours of training per year for every employee**. The total cost for an effective training program is 2 percent of your payroll (40 hours ÷ 2,000 hours per year = 2%). Don't you think you can improve your productivity more than 2 percent by investing in a real training program? Studies show the return on forty hours of training per year can be a 5 to 15 percent improvement in bottom-line productivity. At a 5 percent return, your training program will save 100 hours per employee per year. **WOW! That's real money!**

The Training Table

Training Cost

Average employee cost with fringes	$35 / hour		
Training cost @ 40 hours / year	$1,400 / employee		

Productivity Improvement:	**5%**	**10%**	**15%**
Total hours / year worked	2,000	2,000	2,000
Productivity Improvement @ 5%	100 hours	200 hours	300 hours
Productivity Improvement	$3,500	$7,000	$10,500
Training cost @ 40 hours / year	$1,400	$1,400	$1,400
Net cost saved with training	**$2,100**	**$5,600**	**$9,100**
Total number of employees	10	10	10
Total annual savings	**$21,000**	**$56,000**	**$91,000**

One of my favorite slogans is: **"It's O.K. to improve our company on company time."** The first decision to start an effective training program is to do it on company time, during regular working hours. You can't afford not to train, and it must be a mandatory priority for everyone. Every week (I prefer to train on Tuesday mornings), spend thirty to forty-five minutes training every employee.

Getting started is simple. Have a team meeting to select and prioritize your fifty-two weekly training topics for each company department. List the top fifty-two systems you must do perfectly to build a great company. These are your training topics.

Bosses, Step Back!

In your training program, cover the same basic topics every year, plus the new systems you are implementing, new requirements, topics, and innovative ideas. Conduct your training sessions in an interactive setting (versus the old classroom style of teaching where the teacher simply tells the students what to do). Think coaching versus teaching and telling. Coaches show how, watch their players practice, and then give feedback. In group settings, select different people to lead the weekly training sessions so everyone gets a chance to teach. Assign topics to individuals based on their experience and skill. Use outside instructors when introducing new or technical subjects. Get people to stand up, participate, try the tools, use the equipment, work with the forms, understand the checklists, and do it until they get it right.

Seven Steps to Training Success!

1. Tell people how to do it
2. Show them how to do it
3. Let them do it
4. Watch the results
5. Coach the participants
6. Give feedback and correct mistakes
7. Recognize those who do a good job

Work Together to Learn Together!

Off-site seminars and workshops can be excellent training opportunities as well, but make sure the programs offer more than just listening to an instructor. **Good training involves interaction, doing, coaching, and feedback.** A problem I often see as a speaker is that the agenda of the company I'm visiting includes training sessions led by the business owner, but no real hands-on learning happens. Some companies try to do all their training at one big annual meeting for their entire staff. The employees watch boring technical presentations, or a company manager reads information to the group. The staff doesn't participate in activities or provide input, and therefore doesn't learn how to implement the new skills being taught. They sit there, listen, and try to stay awake. And then, back at work the next day, they continue to do their job exactly as they did before.

I also speak at a lot of annual meetings and conventions where effective learning *does* takes place. Annual meetings can be great training opportunities when combined with ongoing weekly training sessions. Use your annual meetings for real training, feedback, fun, motivation, rewards, excitement, and recognition.

Working together to learn and improve each week fosters team spirit and enthusiasm. Give your people weekly opportunities to perform, to learn, and to train others. The return to your company in productivity, quality work, motivation, and staff loyalty will be exponential. **The end result of an ongoing and effective training program will be no pain and lots of gain!**

Step 4: Build Operational Systems!

Business-Builder Action Plans

1. Decide what ten proactive operational systems are needed in each of your company's departments.
2. Create and install two written systems per month.
3. Manage the systems rather than controlling or doing the work.
4. Set and track targets, productivity, and your numbers.
5. Hold regular, mandatory meetings.
6. Make training a priority and install a training program.

To download the Business-Builder Worksheets, visit:
GetYourBusinessToWork.com/book

step **5**

Build Customer, Marketing, and Sales Systems!

I'm out of town playing golf and my cell phone rings. It's Randy, one of
my best customers. He tells me he has just signed a long-term lease with a
manufacturing company for a new 60,000-square-foot building to be built
in Anaheim, California. Randy then asks me the magic question: "Do you
want to build it for us? If you're interested, you have to attend a prelimi-
nary design meeting tomorrow at 9:00 a.m. at the architect's office. Are
you in?" This is what I call "customer magic"! Our customer systems are
working just the way they're designed to work.

What's Your Customer, Marketing, and Sales System?

Do you have a customer system? A marketing and sales system should get
customers to:

- *Call your company first*
- *Only call your company*
- *Want to do business with your company*
- *Only use your company*
- *Be loyal to your company*

Marketing Is:

- Staying in touch with customers
- Seeking repeat, old, new, and potential customer targets
- Getting the word out about what your company offers or provides
- Creating a perception of your company for potential customers
- Presenting your company image, capability, reputation, and experience
- Developing a market-wide perception that your company is the best choice
- Showing customers that you care about them and their results
- Taking care of your customers and saying thanks
- Sending customers materials to help them
- Helping customers make more money
- Giving customers reasons to want to do business with your company

Marketing Is Not:

- Waiting for customers to call you
- Picking up a set of specifications and turning in proposals
- Calling customers three weeks later to see how your proposals look
- Getting contracts and then arguing about the terms
- Sending out employees who are not trained professionals
- Overbilling for things not yet completed or delivered
- Asking too much money for additional items
- Being under-capitalized and always needing to get paid fast
- Not paying your suppliers or vendors on time
- Promising to deliver on time and then finishing late
- Overcommitting and over-promising on commitments

Sales Is:

- Generating sufficient leads to maintain sales revenue goals
- Proactively calling on leads and targeted customers
- Following up promptly on every lead, proposal, or quote
- Spending face-time with customers
- Convincing customers to buy from your company
- Aggressively asking for orders
- Not waiting for the phone to ring
- Not waiting for customers to show up at your front door
- Giving customers a reason to buy from your company

Sales Is Not:

- Waiting for customers to call you back
- Telling customers what your product or service will cost
- Sending out price lists, catalogs, and brochures
- Showing customers your products
- Explaining what your proposal includes and excludes
- Sending customers e-mails, faxes, and mail
- Giving customers the lowest or discounted price to get them to buy
- Hoping your advertisements bring customers in
- Putting your phone number on your trucks and signs
- Hoping your past customers give you a referral
- Waiting for your past customers to use your company again
- Updating your website

Do You Have a "Loyal Customer" Strategy?

Great marketing and sales systems will consistently deliver profitable work via loyal customers who use your company exclusively. For example, I am a repeat customer of Wal-Mart and Target stores. I will frequent them when it is convenient or if I'm looking for something I want to get at a great price. But I am not *loyal*, because it doesn't really matter to me which chain store I buy my shaving cream from. On the other hand, I am loyal to Bill, my insurance agent. He treats me as if I am special, and provides a customized service designed to give me exactly what I need. I think of him as my business partner. I trust that Bill will always look out for me and my company in every transaction. Because of this, I am *loyal* to Bill, trust he will get me a fair price, and intend to use him forever.

An effective "loyal customer" strategy will increase sales, create profitable customers, earn business at your price, and convert repeat customers to loyal ones. **Is your "loyal customer" strategy working?** Do you turn down more profitable work than you can handle? Are you making more money than your competitors? Is your flow of work steady and predictable? Are you in control of your sales volume? You can count on loyal customers to bring you business because you make them a priority in how you run your business operations. You stay in touch with loyal customers and call or meet with them on a regular basis. Bill meets with me twice a year and calls me every two months to check in and see how our business is doing, if there are any changes, or if we need any other services. He and I have a trusted relationship. I don't have a relationship with anyone at Wal-Mart or Target, even though they are good companies, provide good products, and offer good service.

Over the last twenty years, the economy has created a stress on pricing and profits. There are too many competitors who compete with your company. Most companies, including yours, can do—and want to do—more work with their current resources. This creates too much capacity for the total work available in any marketplace, which causes a downward price pressure and a very competitive work environment. The only way to get lots of work is to price your products and services lower than you want to or should to make enough profit to get a fair return. **In order to increase prices, you need to offer something DIFFERENT than your competitors.** But most companies continue to offer the same things.

For example, does it really matter which dry cleaners you take your shirts and pants to? We used to take our clothes to the lowest priced of the many cleaners within close proximity to our house. Then John, the owner of one of the local dry cleaners, called and offered pickup and delivery for a small extra charge. So now we only use John's company. John always calls in advance to remind us that he will be there on Thursday mornings. He also calls if he will be late or coming on another day. If we won't be home, he makes sure we have a clothes rack outside waiting for his delivery. When it rains, he makes arrangements to put the clothes inside the garage. When we need some hems done, we give him a note pinned to the pants and he returns them the next week, cleaned and shortened. We trust John and now have a relationship with him. By offering a different and more convenient service than his competitors—even though he charged a bit more for it—John made us into loyal customers whom he can count on for lots of annual business.

Ask yourself:

- Why should customers *only* buy from your company?
- Should customers pay more to use your company?
- What do you different than your competitors?

Most companies you compete with probably provide good service, good quality, and good prices. It really doesn't matter to the customers whether they buy from your company or your competitors, because the businesses all operate the same way. When you provide the same service or quality as your competitors, you have little chance to increase your profit margin and a slim chance to hit your bottom-line goals. This allows customers to chart your course. In order to get what you want, you must offer more than your competitors. What do you do to stand out from the crowd and make customers only want to use your company?

Aim for the Edges

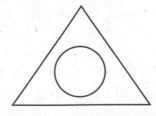

Low Price Leader

Service Leader

Quality Leader

Successful companies find ways to be market leaders by differentiating themselves from their competition. One way to lead is to offer the best price, service, or quality. For example, Wal-Mart and Costco strive to sell for the lowest price. Nordstrom and FedEx offer great customer service. Mercedes-Benz and BMW provide the best products. These companies are market leaders and don't try to be all things to all customers. Either they are the cheapest, the best at service, or the best at quality. They aim for the edges of the triangle. Most small businesses struggle by trying to be all things to all customers: best service, best quality, *and* lowest price. They aim for the middle and compete with everyone else who is also trying to do everything for everybody.

Most entrepreneurs believe in their product and service. They strive to provide the best in their marketplace. Walk into any small bakery or butcher shop and the owner will tell you they offer the best quality in their city. Call any residential real estate sales office and the owner will tell you their agents offer the best service in the area. Call any carpet cleaning service and the owner operator will pride himself on the best workmanship in town. But are they really any better than their competition? In reality, they are providing those great services and products at a very competitive price. They are trying to be the best at everything, which doesn't work. There is no money in competing for the middle of the triangle. But when you are perceived by customers as really being the best at something, you will attract customers who want what your company offers, and then you can charge a premium.

We just had to repair the roof at our home. The job entailed removing the damaged roof at the ridge line, repairing the roof structure, replacing some of the exposed wood ceiling below, re-roofing, and then repainting the entire living room and master bedroom ceiling. Our ultimate goal was a perfectly completed project with the least disturbance to our lives. We needed to hire a roofing company and a painting contractor to complete the job. Price was not really a primary factor for us. We called subcontractors to give us estimates and suggestions for the work needed. We hired our trusted contractor Phil, whom we have used numerous times, to supervise the work. He offers the best service at a fair, but not cheap, price. We hired the best roofer we knew who would keep our house and yard clean and get the job done with the best quality materials and installation. We didn't even ask the roofer for a quote. And we hired Al, the fastest painter in town, who guaranteed us that his crew would finish the entire job in two days.

Guess what? Al's price was also very cheap because he is used to competing on low price to get work. He didn't even know what we wanted or valued before he offered us a bid. And I bet he doesn't make much money trying to be very fast and very cheap. What can you offer customers in your marketplace which will get you more work at a higher price? If you are recognized as the fastest service provider, you should be able to get lots of work from customers who need jobs done quickly, and you should charge a higher price for it. Looking at our choices to repair our roof, we chose a company we trusted to provide the highest quality, since having the lowest price wasn't as important to us as a perfect roof installation. What do you strive to offer to set your company apart as being the best in your market?

An effective marketing program will exploit your differences, maximize relationships with customers, and make potential customers aware of why they should only use your company.

In order to be effective with both your marketing program and sales systems, you must decide what you want your company to compete on:

____ **best service**

____ **best quality**

____ **lowest price**

Without a clear focus on what you provide and what makes your company different, you'll never hit your customer, sales, or bottom-line targets.

Why do you need a written marketing program and sales systems? As business owners, we hire at least 100 different vendors, subcontractors, and service providers to help run our company. These include insurance agents, printers, lawyers, accountants, janitors, architects, landscape designers, civil engineers, bankers, mortgage brokers, real estate agents, mechanical engineers, escrow officers, title insurance agents, website designers, graphic artists, and electrical engineers. As general contractors, we hire hundreds of subcontractors every year, including plumbers, mechanics, fire sprinkler installers, electricians, carpenters, landscapers, earthworkers, concrete layers, masonry workers, ironworkers, drywall installers, painters, cabinetmakers, and pavers. As real estate developers, we hire property managers, real estate brokers, street sweepers, landscape gardeners, cleaning services, and many other vendors.

Thinking of all these companies and businesses we use on a regular basis, it amazes me that **only two or three out of 100 actually do any marketing or sales.** Most don't ever thank us as their customer, show they care, try to keep us loyal, set themselves apart from their competition, or look for ways to improve their service or help us make more money. These 97 percent don't have an ongoing proactive marketing program, a systemized sales plan, updated brochures, a customer-focused website, a referral-generating system, or a program to keep customers wanting more. The norm for these 97 percent is to try and do a good job for their customers and hope they will continue to do more business with them. They don't do any marketing, take customers to lunch, invite customers to ball games, send thank you cards, get together with customers to talk about their service, ask how they could do a better job, keep their customers informed, offer anything more than the minimum required, or hold sales meetings to properly present their companies to their customers.

The top 3 percent of companies that have a written marketing program and use a systemized sales system get more of our work at a much higher price. These top companies set themselves apart from their competition by doing little things that make a big difference. For example, title insurance is a commodity needed to close escrows on real estate projects. Rich is our title representative from one of the large national title insurance companies. He is also one of the top producing salespeople in the country for his company. His marketing program includes inviting me and my wife Alana to a few baseball games every year, bringing me a personalized thank you gift when appropriate, inviting me to play in his foursome in one or two industry golf tournaments every year, and giving me a seat at his table at the big annual industry dinner. His sales system is simple. He visits our office every month to see if we need anything or if he can help out with any problems. He asks what it will take for him to get the order and asks if we have any referrals for him. Guess what? His investment in marketing and selling to our company gives him a big return: he gets all of our title insurance work at the price he charges, no questions asked.

Mark owns a carpet and flooring company, and we are one of his many customers. Mark's marketing program and sales system is simple and it works. To set himself apart and make sure he gets most of our flooring work, he stops by our office at least once every four to six weeks. He checks in with our estimator and project managers to see if he can price any upcoming projects. He follows up in person on his pending proposals, and checks on the progress of every project to be sure he is ready to install when the jobs are ready. Then he does the most important thing to improve his business relationship with our company: he walks into my office, says hello, asks how my family is, checks on my latest golf trip, discusses our vacation plans, asks if I have tried any new wines lately, and then asks me some questions how he can improve his business. By asking for help, he is building a relationship of trust. This is deeper than selling low price. Often he remembers our previous conversation and will bring a sleeve of the latest new golf balls, an interesting bottle of wine, a brochure to a golf resort he has heard about, or a book on great golf holes. In his simple but caring way, he is creating a trusted relationship and showing that he cares about me as a person. This makes me want to tell our project managers to award all of our flooring work to Mark's company.

What Do You Do to Market or Sell?

Generally there are four kinds of companies that compete for more business:

1. Companies that provide the minimum quality required, average service, and get awarded business based on being known as the **lowest price provider**.
2. Companies that provide **excellent quality <u>and</u> service**, count on their reputation to keep customers coming in, but still compete on low price.
3. Companies that are know for providing the **best quality <u>or</u> best service** in the marketplace and get a higher price than most competitors.
4. Companies that provide a good service and good quality workmanship **AND have an ongoing marketing program and sales system to attract profitable customers**, which also get a higher price than most competitors.

Those companies that invest in a small amount of marketing don't have to be the best at what they do to continue to grow and profit at a higher rate than their competitors. On the other hand, those who wait for the phone to ring, don't market or sell, and complain about the economy will always struggle to make enough money to build profitable businesses.

Jared owns a small dredging company in Florida for waterfront property owners who need their docks or beaches dredged after storms or to improve their property. He came to one of my boot camps and I got to know him well. His business plan consisted of owning the biggest floating crane on a barge in his area, putting a sign on it, doing good work at very reasonable prices, and hoping his Yellow Pages ad would keep the phone ringing with new customers.

Jared's business was based on his ability to get the work done. He ran the crane, supervised the crews, paid the bills on the weekends, and answered the phone from his seat on his barge. When a customer called, he would set up an appointment to meet them later that day and give them a price. Like most hands-on business owners, he wasn't making a lot of profit and didn't see the value of a marketing program or selling system. He told me: "I don't need marketing or sales. I stay pretty busy based on doing good work, getting a few referrals, and offering a low price. I printed up some brochures and took out an ad once, but they didn't really do much for business. And besides, I don't have time to take my good customers to lunch, get to know them, and ask for referrals." But he really wasn't getting enough work to make any money, grow his business, or hire the right people to run his business for him.

Without an ongoing marketing program and a systemized sales system, it's impossible to get enough work or sales to maximize your bottom-line and grow your company (*unless your prices are stupid low*).

You have repeat customers who use your company when you're the lowest price provider. But to convert repeat customers into loyal customers takes more time and effort. It takes a systemized approach to building customer relationships. Without an effective marketing program and sales system in place and working, customers run your business. They call you when they need your service or want to buy some of your products, having found out about your company from some random method. They give you their business if they want to, when they want to, at the price they want to pay. When your marketing program or sales system is nonexistent, sporadic, or random, you wait for customers to call or walk into your front door. You are not in charge of your revenue stream, you can't control your future, and you are at the mercy of who says what about your company.

There are only two times when you need to market and sell: when you need more business and when you don't!

Sales is about asking for the order and closing the sale with target consumers.

Marketing is about letting customers know you have something of interest to them, which they ideally can't do without, and getting them to want to buy from you. It is everything you do to promote your business from start to finish, including all customer contacts, impressions, and service. It is making customers aware of what you do, how well you can serve them, and creating the right perception of your company. It is also—and more importantly—creating relationships that reduce the need to hard-sell, negotiate, or cut your price.

Let Customers Know You Have What They Want

Customers want what they want. Not what you have to offer. Most say they want the lowest price, the best quality, and the best service (free, perfect, and now!). But if this was true, everyone would be driving fifteen-year-old Ford Falcons, wearing generic jeans from Wal-Mart, and washing their own cars. People do want a fair price, but they also want to know that what they buy is a good value. And to make it an even better buy, if your product or service is unique or different, customers often forget their desire to obtain the lowest price. Customers want a unique product or service and will pay more for it. Examples: iPhone, BMW, FedEx, Starbucks, Titleist Pro V1 golf balls, my insurance agent, and my flooring contractor.

The choices you can offer customers include:

> **Low price**
> **Perceived value**
> **Differentiation**
> **Trusted relationships**

Changing your prices will increase or lower sales, keep you busy or slow, provide cheap or highly profitable sales, and give customers a perception of your company. If you lower your prices, it will only get you more business if you make your customers aware of your actions.

Improving and increasing the perceived value of your service or product will enhance you position in the marketplace. If you want to be known as the provider of the best quality workmanship, a marketing program outlining why your company delivers precision quality will increase your value to those customers who want perfect quality. Customers will pay a higher or lower price based on *THEIR* perception of your company's service or product's value.

Differentiating your company from your competition is another business option. By offering something more, unique, value-added, or different, you can set your company apart. For example, being perceived as the most creative cake designer in your neighborhood will sell more cakes at a higher price than trying to grow your business by selling average cakes at the lowest price in town. If you are the recognized expert in providing accounting services to doctors and you also offer proven practice building consulting, you will be able to attract more business at a higher price from doctors than most other CPAs who don't specialize.

Building trusted relationships with customers is another excellent way to give them what they want. Some customers want to know who they are doing business with. They want to believe that you will take care of them, treat them right, and give them the best for what they need. Trust is built on friendship and confidence in you and your company. It is not based on providing the lowest price.

Give Customers What They Want!

When your customers call, what do they want? They want you to help them solve their problems. If your marketing program has done an effective job, your customers will know you can supply what they want. So when they call, your sales department should be ready to help them solve their problems. **Companies that have salespeople focused on helping customers increase their odds of getting more profitable sales.** The more you *do for* your customer, the more business you'll *do with* your customer over time. Your job is to discover what your customers need and want, and then deliver it to them.

Show Customers You Care!

The #1 reason customers stop using companies, frequenting businesses, or buying services is because of a perceived attitude of indifference. They don't think you care about them. Over time, companies take customers for granted, don't treat them with respect, and start thinking of them as necessary evils. **Customers stay where they feel appreciated and cared for.** Most companies fail to realize that it takes five to seven times more energy and money to get new customers than to keep existing ones. Most spend more time trying to find new customers instead of working to make their repeat or loyal customers feel wanted and appreciated.

What do you do to show existing customers you care about them and their success? Here are a few ideas.

1. Provide proactive service and quality

- Stay informed of all schedules and deadlines
- Do your own quality assurance
- Stay in touch with customers

2. Provide ongoing customer education

- Provide customer workshops and seminars
- Send out information updates
- Notify customers of all changes to products and services
- Visit customers' operations to review processes
- Send trade magazines and business articles

3. Recommend

- Consultants, attorneys, accountants
- Vendors, suppliers, subcontractors, distributors
- Bankers, lenders, equity sources
- Real estate brokers, title, escrow
- Insurance agents

4. Be a business consultant

- Review customers' systems and operations
- Give customers management ideas

- Provide administrative checklists and forms to use
- Provide accounting and financial tips

5. Help your customers' sales

- Provide leads
- Introduce customers to potential customers of their own
- Network with current and potential customers
- Take customers to association and industry events
- Offer joint marketing programs and mailings

6. Samples and literature

- Stock and restock samples, brochures, and product literature
- Keep customers abreast of new products and services

7. Customer-friendly website

- Be a resource to find information
- Offer tips for better service
- Design a customer-centered website

8. Regularly send things to customers

- Handwritten postcards
- "I Appreciate You" notes
- Thank you cards
- Magazine articles focused on customers' challenges
- New product information
- Samples or guides
- Code or law updates
- Business books to help your customers
- Photos of your services or products
- Greetings
- Postcards while on vacation

Customer loyalty is the result of the quality of your relationship. By helping customers meet their goals, spending quality time with them, and staying in touch, you will improve your top-line success. Every customer has different priorities and areas where you can help them become better businesspeople or improve their lives.

1. *Identify each of your top customers.*
2. *Make a list of what they want.*
3. *Develop your action plan to help them.*
4. *Ask how you can show you care about their success.*
5. *Draft a plan to convert existing customers from first-timers to repeat to loyal.*

A marketing program and sales system can generate a big return for a small investment. Most of your competitors won't invest enough, if anything, on this important part of their business. They figure that if they do a good job, provide a reasonable service, or turn out good products, they'll get lots of customers. This is true, if you want to build your business based on being the low price provider to drive your sales volume. In order to make customers aware of your company's uniqueness and expertise, and to develop loyal customer relationships, you must be willing to dedicate a small amount of time, energy, and money to your marketing program and sales systems.

Marketing and Sales takes time, energy, and money!

Create a Customer-Focused Motto

Start by creating a motto or slogan you can use in everything you send out. For example, my speaking business motto is: "Let's talk about building *your* business!" Our construction company motto is: "Our goal is to help make *your* project a success!" Ford Motor Company's motto is "Service Is Job 1." Customer-focused mottos will set your company apart, as most of your competitors don't have a motto or know what they stand for.

Create a motto focused on what your company *will do* for your customers. Use words that describe how you help your customers' businesses, projects, environment, future, or life when they do business with you. I often see poor customer mottos focused on what the company *has done*, like: "Twenty-nine years of service and quality." This isn't focused on what the company *will do* for the customer, instead stating the obvious: "service and quality." Service and quality aren't differentiating factors to your customers; they are an expected minimum requirement. A better motto would be: "Our twenty-nine years guarantee we'll deliver the extra quality you want and the incredible service you deserve!"

Keep your customer-focused motto consistent. Don't change it often. (Think of Nike's "Just do it"!) Put your motto everywhere—on your business cards, quotations, proposals, invoices, letterhead, front door, website, job signs, trucks, flyers, and brochures.

Become the Recognized Expert

Experts make more money, get the first call from customers, and the last look on their quotations. Are you an expert? What do you specialize in? Do your customers know your expertise? The best way to become an expert in customers' minds is to tell them about your expertise, over and over and over. I once saw a mechanical service truck driving down the freeway, and it had a sign on the door saying: "XYZ Refrigeration Maintenance Company: Commercial – Industrial – Residential." Their sign described them as a "Jack of all trades and a master of none"! I wouldn't call them to work on my house, a hospital, a grocery store, a pizza restaurant, or to repair the air-conditioning on an office building unless I knew what they specialized in. I didn't perceive them as experts. I bet they get most of their contracts by offering low bids on any type of work they can get!

When you start your marketing program, you must decide what you want to become the perceived expert in. More than one expertise is acceptable and often desirable. **But your marketing message must keep focused on what you want to become known for.** We use several different real estate brokers to help us find, lease, and sell our commercial real estate projects. Even though we have trusted relationships with many of them, we specifically choose to hire the real estate expert or specialist for each project based on the project location, type, and building sizes. The successful real estate salespeople and brokers are those who know what they do best and stay focused on that type of product and market. We would never consider hiring the best residential broker to find us ten acres of industrial building land, even if he was my brother-in-law.

The key is to create separate marketing materials that show your company as an expert, specializing in only one type of product or service. **Create separate marketing materials for each of your specialties.** If you run a plumbing company that works on both medical and apartment buildings, create two separate brochures and marketing campaigns focused on the target customers who want what your company offers for each project type. If you run an employment agency that handles placing all types of employees, send out marketing materials focused on targeted industries, like healthcare, manufacturing, or retail services. When I was looking for a literary agent to handle this book project, I sought out agents who knew the business book market versus those who handled bestselling fiction authors. When you try to combine all of your services into one marketing campaign, advertisement, or brochure, you confuse customers looking for a specific type of provider.

You're in the People Business!

Like it or not, you're not in the business you think you're in. No, you're not a lawyer, or a storekeeper, or a bread maker, or a painter, or a business consultant, or a television repair service, or a delivery service, or an advertising agency. **Those who realize they are actually in the people business make lots of money**.

Elyse owns a custom jewelry store that specializes in selling large, expensive diamonds in a beachfront community. She realizes that while she must create incredible pieces of unique jewelry, her real business is getting all of the local women to give her referrals and buy from her. She builds her business by attending and schmoozing at all of the charity events in town, putting on private dinners for the "in crowd," hosting fashion shows, getting involved with all of the upscale women's events in the community, taking potential customers to lunch, meeting women for tea at the mall, and having a drink after work with current and repeat customers. She also sends out at least one thank you note every day, along with pictures of her exquisite diamond jewelry creations. Getting orders is her #1 focus, not making the jewelry. Because of her marketing and sales approach to growing her business, she has developed a trusted relationship with over a hundred women who keep her sales high and give her lots of referrals. Plus she doesn't have to worry about offering the lowest prices to meet her sales goals.

Consider the following fifteen questions about your marketing and sales approach to growing your company.

Business-Builder Worksheet #15

Draft Your Customer-Focused Business Plan:

1. What is our marketing strategy?
2. What is our sales strategy?
3. What do we do to find and attract new customers?
4. What do we do to keep customers?
5. What do we do to get new customers to call?
6. What do we do to differentiate ourselves and stand out from our competitors?
7. What do we proactively do to get lots of referrals?
8. What do we do to thank customers?
9. What do we do to help customers?
10. What is our system to build loyal customer relationships?
11. What do we do to show our top customers we care about them?
12. What do we do to appreciate our best customers?
13. What do we do to stay in touch and schmooze with our customers?
14. What do we do to convert repeat customers to loyal ones?
15. What do we do to treat our best customers in an extra-special way?

No Trust = No Sales!

When you do regular business with customers, you are just doing business as usual. When you get to know your customer in a deeper way, you begin to build trust. The more time you invest in building customer relationships, the more trust you will gain. **When you have customers who trust you, they will want to do business with you and give you referrals.** Trust is built during face-to-face relationship-building sessions. Relationships grow when you are together having fun, enjoying a meal or event, or discussing ways to help each other. This occurs away from day-to-day business activities. Think of close friends. You built your friendships by spending quality time with them and doing lots of fun things together.

Three Steps to Create Trusted Customer Relationships

1. **Familiarity**—quality time getting to know your customers
2. **Awareness**—making customers realize that you care about them
3. **Frequency**—lots of face-to-face time together

To develop trusted relationships, your marketing program must include time with targeted customers in relationship-building sessions. Frequency is the most important factor in building customer relationships.

The More Time Spent Together, the Deeper the Relationship

Years ago our company was trying to win a contract away from one of our competitors. I did everything I could think of to try to get in front of this potential customer, meet him, and start a relationship. But he wouldn't meet with me. When it came time to bid on the work, we decided to go low with our price and hope this would get the customer to finally meet with us and give us the job. After the proposals were sent in, we continued trying to get a meeting with the customer, but to no avail. At an industry event a few days later, I was talking to another business executive and explained our predicament. He asked who the potential customer and competitor was. When I told him, he laughed and told me that we were wasting our time going after that customer. Why? Our competitor was best friends with the customer, attended the same church, sat on two charity boards with him, golfed in the same group every Friday, went on several annual hunting trips with him, and has been doing all of his work for fifteen years. We didn't have a chance trying to break into that long relationship. And to this day, he is still right.

Create a Customer Contact Tracking Chart

In order to make frequent customer contact a priority in your marketing program, use a **Customer Contact Tracking Chart** to keep track of how often you stay in touch with customers, meet face-to-face, have personal relationship meetings, go out to lunch, send marketing materials, send thank you cards or other handwritten notes, e-mail a friendly message, attend industry events together, give personalized gifts, go to a ball game or sporting activity together, play golf, or any other proactive contact that will help build customer relationships or get your marketing message across.

Many companies—such as business-to-business service providers, consultants, contractors, printers, wholesale distributors, and insurance agents—have less than twenty major customers who make up the majority of their business. While other types of companies—like retail stores, consumer services, repair businesses, restaurants, suppliers, real estate brokerages, and employment agencies—can have thousands of customers. These companies with larger customer bases still must sort through their entire customer list to determine who their important customers are and who makes up the majority of their sales volume.

Identify your entire customer target marketing list, including current loyal customers who always use your company, repeat customers who have frequented your company over the last three to five years, new potential customers you want to target in the future, and referring parties who can give your company recommendations.

Rank each customer target by total sales volume, average order size, or profit potential. Then mark an (A) by excellent or loyal customers, a (B) by good repeat customers, a (C) by average customers, a (D) by poor customers, and an (F) by customers you need to stop doing business with. Also rank customers based on the **ROE Factor**, the return on energy it takes to keep them satisfied.

Next, use the Customer Contact Tracking Chart to start tracking your marketing program, customer relationship building, and sales call activity. Keep a **customer information sheet** for every customer with their name, contact information, phone number, e-mail, address, personal facts, and average size order or contract. Also keep a record of their past activity with your company, conversations, proposals, buying habits, special requests, needs, wants, and notes about how they like you to do business with them. For every customer contact, quotation, proposal, contract award or purchase, or outbound marketing activity, record the contact date and exact customer contact type you or your company performed.

Business-Builder Worksheet #16

Customer Contact Tracking Chart				
Customer	$$$	ROE	Contact Type	Month 1 2 3 4 5 6 7 8 9 10 11 12
Loyal				
Repeat				
Potential				
Referring				

Keep track of each of your customer targets and track the following:

$$$ = Rank customer by total sales volume, average order size, or profit potential

    A = Excellent customer—usually very loyal

    B = Good repeat customer who frequents your business

C = Average infrequent customer who often shops for the lowest price

D = Poor customer who gives you grief

F = Bad customer you wish you'd never met and need to stop doing business with

Customer = Customer name and contact information, phone number, e-mail, address, personal facts

ROE = Return on energy to keep customer satisfied (1 = worst; 10 = easiest to keep)

Contact date = Date of customer contact

Customer Contact Type:

FTF M = Face-to-face meeting

FTF CC = Face-to-face cold-call meeting

FTF F = Food or meal with target customer

FTF E = Met or took target customer to event

E = E-mailed target customer to stay in touch

G = Gave personalized gift to target customer

MM = Mailed out marketing materials to target customer

S = Sent target customer a card, note, or thank you

X = Extra or any other customer target contact marketing activity

---

Any Marketing Is Better Than No Marketing!

When you first started your business, you didn't have any customers. So the first thing you had to do was find some. You eventually landed a few customers and got busy doing the work you love to do. Work first, marketing and sales second. The pattern goes:

Work, work, work . . . until you're out of work.
Then find some more work, so you can go back to work.

Eventually your company reaches a plateau and can't grow without some new customers. You need a marketing program and sales system that generates new leads and gets customers to call your company or visit your store. So now what? It's back to the beginning—find new and potential customers to target. In order to market your company's value effectively, you have to start with a target list of customers who are the most likely to need what you have to sell.

I often speak at the National Speakers Association conventions and meetings. After I present my program on how to build your speaking business, many new speakers call me to ask how they can implement their marketing plan and get booked to speak. I ask them two questions:

1. Why should anyone hire you?
2. What's your best target market?

They will tell me they are really good speakers (not different), can speak on a variety of topics (no expertise: Jack of all trades), and work well with most audiences (no target market).

Look at what you want to offer to the marketplace to set yourself apart from your competition. Ask yourself those same two questions. To build a successful business, you've got to give customers a reason to hire (or buy from) your company. And you've got to get focused on customers who want what you have to sell.

Let's starting by creating your marketing message:

- *Why your company?*
- *Why should customers only buy from you?*
- *What do you do for your customers that no other company does?*
- *What value do you offer to your customers?*
- *What are you the best at (service, quality, or price)?*

In order to project a marketing message to potential customers, you need a unique statement that clearly explains the value you offer your customers. Do you provide the best service, best quality, or lowest price? What is different about your company—service, quality, price, or delivery method? What can you tell potential customers to entice them to call you first? Nordstrom constantly reinforces unquestionable customer service in their marketing. McDonald's talks about a "happy place" and has "Happy Meals" for children. Burger King lets you "Have it your way." "Diamonds are forever." Range Rover is "Designed for the extraordinary." BMW is "The ultimate driving machine." Westin Hotels tells us, "This is how it should feel."

Step 1 is to decide "Why your company?" Only then you can start your marketing program. Create the perception of value you want your customers to remember about your company's services or products. Value is a combination of what you have done in the past, your current capabilities, and what you will do for your customers.

Step 2 is to determine your target market. Before you start making a customer target list, you must decide what type you can serve best, where you want to do business, the perfect customer for you, how you want to do business, and how big you want to become.

Scott owns a computer and software service company. He was doing a pretty good job growing his company until he reached ten service technicians. At that level he couldn't keep up with the many diverse type of customers his company had contracts with. His business consisted of over 200 accounts, ranging from $200 to $3,000 per month, in every type of industry he could land. But as his company grew, the varied customer types had unique and different problems only he could solve. This put a roadblock on his growth and profitability.

He made a strategic business decision to stop working on accounts in all but three industries, raised his minimum monthly fee to $1,000, and eliminated all customers who were more than 60 miles from his office. He stopped advertising in the newspaper and now focuses his marketing efforts on getting referrals from his loyal customers plus target marketing in the three industries he works in. He got involved in their trade associations, takes two customers to lunch every week, and sends out informational postcards to everyone on his target customer list every month. This overall business change allowed his company to reduce the number of accounts, get focused, become an expert in three industries, and since there are so few customer types, it allows him to train his technicians better. Two years later he has twenty-five technicians, is making a lot more net profit, and actually has more time off.

Business-Builder Worksheet #17

Determine Your Customer Business Focus:

1. What type of customers can we serve best?
2. What type of customers need what we offer?
3. What is our perfect customer like?
4. What type of customers can we help the most?
5. Where is our perfect customer base?
6. Where do we want to do business?
7. How do we want to do business? (Wholesale, retail, hourly, contract, etc.)
8. How big do we want to be? (Company, customers, orders, contracts)

Step 3 is to create a target customer list. Complete the Customer Contact Tracking Chart. Identify all of the customers you have done business with over the past three to five years. Sort them by loyal and repeat and rank them in order of potential business. Next, develop a list of all the targets you want to go after in the future. To build your list, you may have to research customer targets using the internet, industry lists, zip codes, by household income, magazine subscribers, etc. If you put your mind to it, you can generate a target customer list in a few days. Don't forget to include your referring parties. For example, in my construction business, referring parties include bankers, lawyers, architects, engineers, subcontractors, real estate brokers, and association members I meet at conventions. Don't discount people you meet. You never know who will refer you some business some day.

Marketing Tactics, Tools, and Tips

Now you can develop a marketing program and determine how you'll attack your target customer list. Start by developing a marketing budget. The right amount will not be based on your annual sales volume. Check your industry standards to see what other successful companies spend to attract profitable customers. In some industries, your company may only need $10,000 per year in marketing expenses to create a minimal marketing program. Other industries will require 3 to 5 percent or more of your total sales to attract enough customers for your business to be profitable. But any amount is better than none!

Mass marketing to thousands of potential customers is expensive. This type of marketing includes advertising in magazines and newspapers, mailing to an entire zip code, buying television spots, billboards, or a trailing sign behind an airplane. While mass marketing can be effective, the return on cost can be very low, as only a small percent of the audience actually needs or wants what you are selling.

Direct target marketing is less expensive and can be more effective because is only aims at your target customer list. Direct target marketing can include taking your top ten customers to lunch or a ball game, manning a booth at an industry trade show, speaking at a conference, sending helpful articles or brochures to your mailing list, sending thank you cards and customized gifts to loyal customers, or sending a monthly top-ten business tips list to your e-mail newsletter subscribers.

Before you start spending marketing money, decide what you want to invest in based on the return you might get. I recently spoke at a large, privately owned Mexican company wanting to expand their business into the United States. To implement their goal of growing their business internationally, they had promoted a manager to vice president of sales. At our meeting he asked me if he should buy pens with the company name and logo on them as a marketing tactic. I asked him if he thought that would get any potential customers to call and give them any work. The answer was obvious: "No!" We decided the best way for them to start attracting new customers was to attend several large industry trade shows, man a booth, work the crowd to generate interest in their services, get leads, and then make appointments to go and see potential customers to present their company's value.

Your goal is to generate the highest return on your marketing money. If your company serves a small number of customers, the highest return is to spend lots of time with your best customers. Take them to lunch every two months. Give them birthday, anniversary, and thank you gifts. Send them handwritten notes with pictures of things they are interested in or tips on new ways to make more money. Invite them to ball games or hunting trips with you. Subscribe to magazines for them. If they golf, give them a dozen of the best golf balls they like twice a year. If they like flowers, subscribe them to the flower-of-the-month club. Take them to industry, charity, or cultural events with you. Get to know them and show them you care about them as people. For the rest of your customer targets on your Customer Contact Tracking Chart, you must keep in contact on a regular basis. Send them a postcard, article, photo, brochure, or flyer at least once every four months. Keep your message focused, using your marketing motto as your overall theme. Tell them why they should do business with your company, and give them a reason to call your company first.

To get the highest return on your marketing dollars is a tougher task if your company serves a large number of targeted customers. Not only does it cost more total dollars to market, it is harder to get potential customers' attention. With your top customers, you should still attempt to build relationships via personal contact as described above. Show your loyal repeat customers you care about them and appreciate their business by using special invitations, lunches, discounts, offers, clubs, events, or receptions. Give these good customers a reason to continue frequenting your business and giving your company referrals. For the rest of your target customer list, constant reminding is required to grow your business. The marketing options are many and expensive, including door hangers, newspaper coupons, mailings, advertising, website placement programs, and billboards. Whether you choose to mail a postcard to every customer in your zip code or take out an ad in your industry trade magazine, be sure to track the results and calls you get from each marketing activity.

The goal of your marketing program is to:

1. Create a perception of value
2. Build trust
3. Reinforce customer relationships
4. Pique customers' interest
5. Get customers off price
6. Get customers to call

1. Create a perception of value by letting customers know why they should hire your company or buy only from you. Tell them your story. Show them your capabilities. Inform them what you'll do for them. Let them know what you are the expert in. Tell them why your product or service will enhance their life or business. Give them a list of past clients to justify their selection of your company. Offer them a report giving them the answers they need to solve their problem. Convince them you are the best choice. Show them pictures of what you have done, what you can do for them, and how you can solve their problems.

2. Build trust by contacting customers over and over again. Don't give up. Trust is built over a long period of time. Marketing is not a one-time event, lunch, meeting, advertisement, or brochure. It takes a diligent, concentrated program to slowly build trust. Your goal is to see your top customers every two to three months. This will ensure that you maintain trusted relationships that will result in you getting a majority of their business. The balance of your customer list should be contacted at least every three months via the mail or other media. Send something out to your entire list to keep your company on their mind. This will show you care and get them to call, refer, or buy from you when the need arises.

In 1995 I made a list of 500 target customers to pursue to build my professional speaking business. My marketing program was simple: mail the entire target list a marketing piece four times every year until they buy or die. I now regularly get calls from people on the target list wanting me to speak at their company or association convention. When asked why they want to hire me, they say they feel like they know and trust me since I have been diligent in mailing them for ten plus years. I was the only speaker who didn't give up! **Marketing is simple: time and a little bit of money.** With your loyal repeat customers, get to know them personally in relationship-building sessions. With your mass-target customers, time and diligence is what will build trust.

3. Reinforce customer relationships by showing customers you care about them and their business or well-being. Rather than spending all of your marketing money taking out ads or sending out brochures and fly-ers that say HIRE US! or BUY FROM US, **offer something that will help your customers**. An engineering company could send out the latest code changes affecting their customers every year. A commercial mortgage bro-ker might hold industry forums twice a year with speakers presenting on the economy and industry trends. A small bank can host networking ses-sions for their customers to meet, greet, and talk about working together to maximize profits. A local auto mechanic could hold clinics for their customers every quarter on how to keep cars running in tip-top shape. An accountant might send out a monthly white paper report on ten ways to improve your business. A flower shop owner can send her customer list quarterly suggestions for making their homes stay fresh and look more col-orful. What could you do to reinforce your customer relationships?

4. Piquing customers' interest is fun and gets lots of attention. An example is the funny or crazy Super Bowl television ads we all wait for every year. My monthly "Hardhat Headlines" e-mail newsletter used to only include my business-building articles and tips. Eventually I added a section on my personal life, fun photos of our trips, some jokes or humor, and action photos of customers at my speaking engagements. Now the response has taken off, the number of new subscribers grows every month, and the number of un-subscribers is almost nonexistent. What can you do to pique your customers' interest? An auto repair business might send out "wreck-of-the-month" before and after photos on postcards to its customer list. A sandwich shop can have a quarterly contest asking for ideas for new sandwiches with unique names. A lawn service could have a monthly newsletter for its customers that includes a joke of the month. Rather than sending a standard holiday card every year, an accountant I know sends out cards from his exotic vacation spots. The cards feature a picture of himself having fun along with the caption: "Having fun investing the money you trusted us to manage!" Guess what? This gets your attention and makes you remember him! I once sent out a hammer and nails to potential customers with a handwritten note: "When can we hammer out our next contract and nail down the terms?" Fun and crazy are good ways to pique your customers' interest.

5. Getting customers off price should be one of your goals when creating your marketing program. The more customers know your company and what you will do for them, the more they will trust you, and the more they will want to do business with you. Price can often become secondary to the relationship. Constantly reinforce how you will meet your customers' needs and help them get what they want. Do home remodel customers want the lowest price or piece of mind? Does a business owner getting sued by an irate customer or employee want the cheapest lawyer or a positive outcome with the least amount of grief? Do you want the cheapest website developer or the one who will get your company the most traffic? Does a Porsche buyer want the cheapest car or the best-looking dates? By focusing your message on your customers' ultimate goal, you can sell them what they really want.

6. Get customers to call, wanting what you have to offer. Many marketing programs create the right image and perception of a company but don't get customers to call. If you spend all your marketing money on uniforms for your employees, keeping your facility spick and span, and doing excellent work, you may not achieve your marketing goal (more revenue at a higher price). Don't forget to ask for the order! How often have you had a vendor submit you a price and never follow up? Often! Most salespeople *never* ask for the order. They figure if they are nice, that should get customers to buy. But most sales occur on the fifth, sixth, or seventh call. Your marketing program must include materials, reasons, and requests for customers to call now.

Minimum Money = Maximum Return!

Remember, the goal of contacting your customers is to get them to call you. Stay in touch by sending customers things that help them grow their business. Mail magazine articles, newsletters, brochures, flyers, reports, invitations, fun things, postcards, tips, or checklists. These ideas can be created quickly, with little expense. In our company, we focus our marketing program first on our top twenty-five to fifty repeat customers, potential customers, and referring parties on the Customer Contact Tracking Chart. Our annual budget is around $200 per target customer to maintain these top relationships, keep them loyal, get them off price, and get them to call only us. This part of our annual budget totals only $10,000 for the cost of special mailings, events, ball games, personalized gifts, and lunches. And that $10,000 returns us over $40 million in sales! For the rest of the thousand targets on our Customer Contact Tracking Chart, our marketing program budget is $2.50 per target customer per quarter, totaling $10,000 per year. This includes only hard costs, not personnel expenses or advertising. This is a great investment and a small price to pay to ultimately create loyal customers who will pay us top dollar to do their work. Marketing systems are simple to maintain and will generate big results. All it takes is a commitment to do it!

Musts to Make More Money

What is the #1 business tactic you must do every day to guarantee you'll make money in good times and bad?

_____ Schedule employees

_____ Price products and services

_____ Purchase materials

_____ Train employees

_____ Collect money

_____ Provide quality workmanship

_____ Provide excellent service

_____ Maximize operational efficiency

_____ Spend less than you make

_____ Know and track your numbers

_____ Find and keep customers

What was your answer? **The #1 most important business tactic required to make a profit is to** *find and keep customers!* Without customers, everything else is irrelevant.

Is Your Customer #1?

What's the common thread for these businesses?

Pebble Beach golf course
Consulting firm
Hilton Hotels
Wholesale paper distributor
Concrete contractor
Symphony orchestra
Manufacturer's representative company
Home builders
Carpet cleaner
Microsoft
The Anaheim Ducks (2007 Stanley Cup winner!)

The answer? **None of them can exist without customers.**

Last year I participated in a major national charity golf tournament. The golf was fine but the player experience, prizes, food, gifts, and quality were not up to par. Even though I believed in the charity's cause, I and several other players told the event organizers we wouldn't be back without major improvements. Our time is valuable, and if we're going to dedicate an entire day to a golf tournament, it had better be first class. There's too much competition even for charity dollars today. Guess what? They listened and upgraded every aspect of the tournament. I attended this year and it was a great, fun experience. Even charities with great causes must put their customers first in order to be successful.

Businesses that are recognized as the best in their markets continually take care of their customers in everything they do. They proactively market their services, sell what they have to offer, nurture new customer targets, create loyal customer relationships, get involved in industry and community organizations, offer differentiating services to customers, and work hard to put customers first. And guess what? They also make more money than their competitors.

Many companies have gotten used to providing mediocre service, using poor business practices, and not marketing to their customers. If a restaurant or hotel operated like most businesses do, it wouldn't stay in business more than a few weeks. In restaurants or hotels, customers won't tolerate poor service, untrained or grumpy employees, unclear expectations, late deliveries, bad quality, lukewarm food, unstocked wine shelves, or excuses. Customers just won't show up or come back. But for 95 percent of all companies, not being proactive toward serving customers has become standard operating procedure. It seems like most companies' customer mottos are: **"No worse than our competition!"** Or: **"If our competitors don't do it, why should we?"**

Marketing and Sales Musts

These marketing and sales musts are simple to implement. They'll make you lots of money and allow you to build better businesses with better customers. But if you don't do some or all of them, your company will stay at the same level and continue fighting for cheap customers.

My Written Marketing and Sales Plan

1. Target Marketing

The easiest and most important thing you must do is to create trusting relationships with your top customers who make you most of your money and pay your bills. Start by making a list of your top customers. Look at every purchase, order, job, or contract you have completed or proposed in the last three to five years. Identify the customer, plus any referring parties like a consultant, engineer, broker, project manager, purchasing agent, or any other person who might have influenced the decision to buy from or hire your company. Also list any potential or customer targets you want to go after in the next few years. List all of these customer targets, potential customers, and referring parties on your Customer Contact Tracking Chart.

Next, rank and sort target customers by these important factors:

Profit potential
Ease of doing business
Desire to do new business
Ease of getting on their bid list
Competitive factors or competition
Ease of negotiating work
Potential to become a repeat customer
Ability to convert from repeat to loyal customer

Now you have a customer target list to begin your sales program. Where should you invest the most time and money? In most businesses, the biggest bang for your buck is creating customer relationships with your top repeat and loyal customers. The next most desired are potential customers and quality referring parties who refer your company lots of business.

2. Constant Customer Contact

To stay in touch with your entire customer list, you must contact every target on your entire customer list at least every three to four months. This will keep you at the top of their minds when they have a need for your products or services. One easy way to perform this task is to assign someone in your company this responsibility. In smaller companies, bring in a college marketing student to help you for a few days every month. Have them create mailing pieces, get them printed, stuffed into envelopes, and mailed. Constant customer contact should accomplish at least one of the following strategies:

A. *Make customers aware of why they should hire or buy from your company*

- Send brochures, flyers, or photos showing your expertise
- Send reports and tips to help customers
- Send announcements of past accomplishments
- Send pictures and résumés of key people
- Participate at industry meetings or panels

B. Create a perception of your company's value

- Show how you accomplish big tasks
- Speak at industry or community events
- Send charts and graphs of your value-added services
- Send photos of your capabilities, products, and services

C. Pique customers' interest so they will remember your company

- Send fun stuff that gets a reaction
- Send unique postcards, greetings, and holiday cards
- Send jokes or cartoons

D. Reinforce your relationships

- Take customers to meals, events, or meetings
- Send personal handwritten notes (one a day!)
- Send photos of order progress
- Send thank you cards after customer contact

E. Show customers you care about their success

- Send magazine articles that help them
- Send tips and guides to help them do things better
- Send books to help customers
- Send ideas to improve customers' lives or businesses

3. Referral Program

Want to double your business? Ask every one of your customers for a referral next week. When visiting or contacting customers, always ask for referrals. Give them an incentive to refer you. This will ensure a consistently growing quality customer target list to use to expand your customer base. Remember, don't ask, don't get! After someone gives you a referral, send a thank you note and a gift as appreciation for their help.

4. Website

Either do your website right or don't waste your time. Your website must show what your company does best. It must demonstrate why your company is the best, what types of services, products, projects, or customers you specialize in, and where your company does business. It must also be a resource center to help your customers solve their problems. Use quality photos, professional graphics, and good links to other sites. Include a homepage, business profile, competitive advantages, your expertise and specialties, client list, corporate team, key management résumés with product or project photos, service photos, testimonials, and a detailed research center for customers to use.

5. Company Brochure

The website criteria apply here as well, except don't waste money on huge twenty-page brochures. Create several small tri-fold brochures or 8½ × 11 flyers for each product, service, customer, or project type you specialize in. Then have customized digital pages ready when you call on potential customers. The days of big expensive brochures are over. Spend the cash on your website!

6. Get Active in Your Industry, Associations, and Community

People want to do business with people they know. A great way to get known is to be active in your industry, associations, and community. Join organizations where your customers hang out and will see your involvement. And get involved by volunteering to chair committees, get on the board of directors, lead the golf tournament, or host the annual fundraiser. The more you're seen doing good things and helping out, the more people will see the good in you, and call on you to help them out. Decide where you'll get the most bang for your buck and join today.

7. Image and Promotional Items

Rule #1: Don't give out junk!

Rule #2: Don't talk to the monkey when you are selling to the organ grinder!

I see lots of companies fall in love with giving out cheap t-shirts, throwaway pens, ugly calendars, and useless notepads. **Don't waste your money on things people will throw away!** After every charity golf tournament or trade show I attend, I leave with a bag of expensive junk that I trash as soon as I get home. Don't waste your hard-earned money on giving useless stuff to the wrong people. Save it up and invest in season tickets to your local ball team and take your top customers out with you. Has your customer's production worker, who is wearing your company logo t-shirt or baseball hat, ever awarded a big contract to your company?

8. Advertising

Placing ads in newspapers or magazines is expensive for businesses serving their local markets. You are investing lots of cash aimed at lots of people who don't need or want what you sell. Advertising has its place for major suppliers of tractors, large national product providers like Ford Motor Company, national service companies like H&R Block, and other types of businesses. But be cautious with your marketing budget. Don't think advertising will keep your pipeline full of profitable customers or work unless you have a big pocketbook. I successfully use advertising in specific industry trade magazines to sell my books, speaking services, and business-owner boot camps. But these are targeted to and focused on a specific audience. If you decide to invest in advertising, make sure it is targeted to customers who need your products and services. You'll get a good return by improving your image and promoting your company in a consistent manner. Invest in unique signs and awesome-looking store and office interiors. Use marketing materials that stand out, have bright company uniforms, and drive clean, professionally painted vehicles.

Now Go Make It Happen!

These marketing and sales musts will make you lots of money! To get started, begin with the method you think will give you the biggest return. For many, your #1 Must-Do should be building relationships with your repeat and loyal customers. This will give you the highest return for your investment of time and money. If you take two customers per week to lunch, fifty weeks per year, you'll only need to budget between $5,000 to $15,000, depending on your taste in restaurants. This is small potatoes compared to making another $50,000 to $100,000 on your bottom-line by working for loyal and repeat customers rather than attracting all your work by being the lowest price provider.

Next, implement the second method you think will give your company the next highest return. For many it will be constant customer contact. If your complete mailing list comprises 500 direct customer targets and you mail to them four times per year at the cost of $2.50 per piece, your investment will only be $5,000 per year. You **WILL** get a return on this marketing effort.

Then decide which other Must-Dos will give you the greatest return. Some companies will need a professional website, others will need a company brochure, and others will be able to get lots of referrals. Choose what will work for you and make it happen! **Remember, any marketing plan is better than a perfect plan that is never executed.**

Step 5: Build Customer, Marketing, and Sales Systems!

Business-Builder Action Plans

1. Develop a "loyal customer" strategy.
2. Offer something different than your competitors.
3. Determine what to market and sell: best service, best quality, or lowest price.
4. Develop a program to create a perception of added value your customers will remember.
5. Find ways to show customers you care about and appreciate them.
6. Create a program to build loyal, trusted customer relationships.
7. Come up with a customer-focused motto based on what you *will do* for them.
8. Become the recognized expert.
9. Draft your Customer-Focused Business Plan. (Worksheet #15)
10. Create a Customer Contact Tracking Chart. (Worksheet #16)
11. Determine why customers should buy from your company.
12. Determine your target market.
13. Determine your Customer Business Focus. (Worksheet #17)
14. Create a target customer list.
15. Develop your written marketing and sales plan.

To download the Business-Builder Worksheets, visit:
GetYourBusinessToWork.com/book

step **6**

Build People and Leadership Systems!

How many times have you said to yourself:

"Nowadays workers just don't care."
"Can't anyone take some initiative?"
"No one accepts any responsibility except me!"
"It seems like people don't get excited about doing a good job anymore!"
"If only we could find some decent help!"

At the same time, your employees are thinking:

"They don't know how to run this place!"
"They never give me any authority to get the job done right!"
"They tell us what to do and then change their minds!"
"I feel like a number around here!"
"I do all the work, and they make all the money!"

Think about that while you read on.

Leaders Lead!

When you hear the word "leader," do you think of a political leader, business leader, financial leader, or yourself? Most small business owners and managers think of themselves as hard workers instead of leaders. Leadership has nothing to do with working hard, setting a good example, or owning a company. **Leadership is your ability to get people to want to follow you.** Leaders get results through people who achieve bottom-line targets. When asked, most business owners think they're great leaders. But most employees say their bosses aren't good leaders at all.

Business owners have a tough job managing customers and working with people to get the results they want. But until they step up to leadership, they won't realize the full potential of their people or company. Most business owners spend far too much time doing the wrong things well. They're great at doing work tasks, which causes them to focus on doing what they're comfortable with instead of doing what makes the most money or produces the highest returns.

Take the Leadership Priority Test

My current time commitments and priorities are:

Doing work	_____ hours per week
Controlling and directing work	_____ hour per week
Managing and supervising people	_____ hours per week
Selling and customer relationships	_____ hours per week
Leading and inspiring people	_____ hours per week
Seeking business opportunities	_____ hours per week
TOTAL work	_____ hours per week

Leadership = Quality and Service = More Sales = Higher Profits

When I present my keynote speech entitled **"You Can't Get Rich With Your Head in a Ditch!"** at conventions, I ask attendees: "Where do successful business owners spend their time, working out on the job site, in their offices, or at the country club?" *The right answer is the country club.* Successful business owners focus on maximizing customer relationships and seeking better business opportunities. This can't be accomplished by doing or micromanaging work. Leaders realize that to hit their goals, they must spend the majority of their time being a leader, not a worker.

Successful business owners who move from a micromanaging role into a leadership one can build successful companies. Effective leaders spend only 25 percent of their time doing work and the other 75 percent leading people, working with customers, seeking better business opportunities, and looking for innovative solutions. When you spend most of your time focused on the work, you forget about what it takes to grow your business.

Amanda owns a bookkeeping service that assists small companies for a few hours or a couple of days every week to manage their accounting needs. Her company has twenty accounts and five employees. She was, of course, the best bookkeeper in her small company, and her clients always wanted her to service their accounts. As she tried to grow her business, she couldn't be at all places at all times, and had to rely on her other bookkeepers to work with some of her clients. She was also worried that as her business grew, her clients would get used to her employees and they might steal business and accounts away from her. She was so busy doing bookkeeping for clients, and checking in on all of her accounts to make sure they remained happy, that she didn't have enough time to focus on anything else. As Amanda became more stressed out, she got very temperamental with her employees. Eventually one of her bookkeepers quit to start her own company, and another gave notice that he was leaving in two weeks. Amanda was now overloaded and out of control. When potential new clients called, she didn't even have enough time to return their calls, go meet with them, or give them proposals. She was stuck at her ability to do and control the work. Now what: shrink, grow, or do something different?

Amanda thought the problem was that her employees were not as dedicated to her customers as she was. But her real problem was the inability to keep the best people motivated to work for her. She hadn't put any time into training her staff, building teamwork, praising or encouraging them, setting clear targets and goals for them to hit, developing a rewards and incentive program to keep them motivated, or meeting with them to discuss their future at her company. Amanda focused on doing the work while she did in her employees! To continue to grow her company, she had to fix this problem. And the fix had to start with Amanda. She had to change her priorities, time, style, focus, and daily activities. She had to become the leader and not the #1 worker and controller.

Talent must be a top priority to hit your company goals. Make it a company goal to become the "employer of choice" and build a great place to work that attracts, trains, and retains the best people in your industry.

Are People Your Top Priority?

As your business grows, set goals and begin to make a profit by installing management, financial, marketing, and operational systems. The next logical step in your Business $uccess Blueprint is to create people, leadership, management, and training systems to get the employees in your business to work the right way for you.

Your talent must become your top priority. The competition for talent is fierce, and your only solution is to

Perfect operational systems won't work without perfect people!

become the "employer of choice" and build a great place to work that attracts, trains, and retains the best people in your industry. Imagine for a moment that you're looking for work as a carpenter in the construction industry. Does this help wanted ad attract you?

Construction Help Wanted

Experienced carpenters needed now. Bring your tools and drive your own truck. Some days it will be freezing cold and others hotter than hell. The job starts at 6:00 a.m. and ends when we run out of work. Most days you'll be dirty, messy, and working in dangerous conditions. You'll do heavy lifting and get really tired. When we're slow, we'll send you home without pay. When it rains or snows—too bad; we'll send you home until the site is ready to start work again, also without pay. We'll train you, but you'd better do it our way. The pay is average and as you get older, you'll become less valuable and might be replaced by a younger or faster person if you can't keep up or start complaining.

We are desperate to hire some good help. So give us a call today and apply for this job—maybe you'll qualify and get it!

Remember your first job? When you were hired, you were excited and really wanted to do a good job. You respected your boss and were willing to do anything asked of you. What happened over the next few months? **Employees lose their enthusiasm as they get to know their boss and are not treated properly**, are taken for granted, are not given proper tools, are given unclear directions, are not allowed to offer any input into decisions, are told what to do, and are treated like hired hands. This causes good employees to act poorly. Then the boss complains he can't find any good help!

The people who work for you are not machines. They need to be treated as the individuals they are. They have lives, families, dreams, and priorities other than work. Remember the old management style? Managers do all the thinking, supervisors do all the talking, and workers do all the doing. The manager's job was to keep people busy, while the worker's job was to do as little as possible while looking busy. This old management style never really worked, and it definitely doesn't work today. Yet it's still being used by struggling small business owners and entrepreneurs who think they are the only one who can think, have any brains, or do things right!

What Do People Want?

The difference in winning sports teams is usually the coach, not great players. Successful managers install systems to coach, train, empower, motivate, and encourage their people. During exit interviews, most employees say they don't get enough recognition from their boss and if they were given more appreciation and respect, they would work harder and do more.

Today's employee wants:

- meaningful and satisfying work
- accountability and responsibility
- pay for performance
- engaging and invigorating assignments
- upwardly mobile work
- a better quality of life

Now, you know this, but I'm going to say it anyway: Employees are not as loyal as their fathers and grandfathers were. They know that by changing jobs, they can make more money, find better opportunities, become challenged, have more fun, and do more rewarding work.

Employees are loyal to their bottom-line, not yours!

Younger employees don't trust their bosses, prefer informal arrangements, need teamwork, want to participate in decisions, need to be informed and involved, expect continuous learning and a high-tech workplace, and want balance in their life. According to a study of Microsoft's employees, 50 percent say they would give up some pay for more time off.

What would your employees say about you as their boss? Are they proud to work for your company? Do they have some control? Do they believe they can make a difference? Do they have freedom from micromanagement? *People don't leave companies, they leave bosses.* A great employee success system will improve profitability, customer service, and employee retention, and reduce stress. A great place to work has an exceptional working environment where people want to produce results.

Hire Slow and Fire Fast

Do you have employees you wish you'd never heard of? Do you have employees whose purpose seems to be to make your life miserable? How did they end up at your company? Generally, poor performing or problem employees are a result of hiring too fast when companies are desperate to fill slots. **The management style of hiring quickly and trying to fix them later doesn't work.** Employees are too often hired based on what you *hope* they can do, regardless of their résumés. Then they're put into jobs without proper indoctrination and with little training, and they're left alone to learn on the job without feedback or coaching.

My business had grown to 150 employees in only seven years. We were at the highest level of my control possible, and our company was starting to self-destruct in every direction. Plus, it was starting to cost us lots of money. I needed help fast. So I drafted the perfect organizational chart to manage and grow our company. I then realized that my name was in six of the top boxes. I was the owner and president, and the acting vice president of business development, estimating, construction, field concrete, finance, and administration. While there were people handling some of the duties in each of those VP positions, I was the one totally accountable and responsible for achieving the results and getting things done. I decided to make some big changes and hire or promote six people into those slots to help our company get organized and back in control so we could continue to grow.

The interview and hiring process was brutal. I got frustrated taking time to interview enough people properly and do in-depth background checks on the top candidates. I wanted to fill the slots quickly and move on to doing my job. So I hired people I thought could do the job well enough, even though their résumés and qualifications didn't exactly fit the positions. Guess what? Out of the six people hired during my hasty selection process, only two lasted more than a year with our company. Only two out of six! The trouble caused by hiring, training, trusting, pushing, and eventually eliminating four managers caused lasting damage to our company for several years. All because I didn't take the time to hire the right people.

Even with a proper interview system using scripted questions, detailed reference checks, résumé reviews, and personality testing, I found you won't hire the right person every time and you are lucky if you get it right 50 percent of the time. (Better than two out of six!) Most companies don't have recruitment or hiring systems in place to help improve their odds of hiring the right person.

What Do You Do to Attract Great Employees?

You can't hire people who don't apply and aren't recruited. The old way of analyzing candidates was to take out an ad, look for experience, hold a quick interview, and hire fast. But that no longer works.

Successful employers know that to find the right employees, they need to slow down and look for:

- determination and drive
- talent and potential
- ability to perform
- consistency and responsibility
- personal life in order

- self-motivation
- teamwork and competitiveness

When reviewing potential employees, look for signs of personal responsibility. Ask them if they own a car or home, or have a family. Seek teamwork and competitiveness from people who played high school sports or continue to play some sort of competitive sports. Look for talent and potential by asking about life accomplishments and school activities. Ask questions about their personal finances to see if they know how to make good decisions. When interviewing, you often want people to be the right employee so badly, you only listen for the right answers instead of the real truth. **Hire attitude and aptitude, and then train skills.**

How to attract great people:

1. Decide that recruiting is everyone's job
2. Make recruiting an ongoing, company-wide event
3. Pay employees to refer potential new hires
4. Offer signing bonuses to new hires
5. Have company recruiting brochures available
6. Have recruiting business cards made
7. Make it easy for recruits to apply
8. Use phone interviews for quick pre-qualification
9. Have a regular weekly interview time
10. Create a simple one-page application
11. Offer gifts or incentives to applicants
12. Ask suppliers and customers to help find candidates
13. Hold monthly career workshops
14. Get involved at high school employment fairs
15. Offer summer jobs to potential employees
16. Offer training on Saturdays
17. Hold career days at your office, shop, or store
18. Offer scholarship programs
19. Let recruits visit your factory, job sites, or other locations
20. **Build a great place to work**
21. **Become the employer of choice**

Motivate People to Perform

Years ago, I went through fourteen secretaries in two years. I just couldn't find anyone who would work as hard as I wanted. No one was ever quick enough, smart enough, or good enough. Plus, none of them could read my mind and make the decisions I expected them to. One day I finally realized that maybe the problem was me! I had to realize that it was my responsibility to lead and inspire my staff. It wasn't their job to motivate themselves. Once I realized that, my personnel problems turned around, our people became great, and our employee retention moved above 90 percent every year. **I had been the problem, not them.**

Are YOU Your People Problem?

To motivate your workforce, you've got to give them a reason to be motivated. People are motivated for *their* reasons, not yours. Don't expect others to understand your passion for customers, or quality work, or the need to make a profit. They must want to follow *your* vision, achieve *your* goals, and get the job done properly.

For example, think of your children. You tell them what you want them to do, but they don't always follow your wishes. Then you try to bribe them— $100 for an A on their report card. They say, "Not enough, Dad." Frustrated, you scream, "If you're not home by 10:00 p.m., I'm going to kill you!" Well, you don't. You let them off the hook and they continue to push the envelope. The real problem is lack of accountability and responsibility. It seems like the problems you have with your kids are the same with your employees.

> **Supervising and managing employees is exactly like being a parent.**

Do Your People Want to Follow You?

Leaders influence others to want to do what they want them to do. The key words are **want to do**. Employees must want to do what you want them to do, to get the results you want. You tell them, and they decide if they'll do it. When you tell your kids to clean up their room, they decide if they'll do it based on the needs, consequences, accountabilities, and responsibilities that affect their decisions.

Ask yourself: "What makes employees want to follow me?" You know what *doesn't* work with your children (and employees)—confusion, lack of trust, no integrity, no accountability, and no consequences. A lot of business owners and managers say, "My people won't do what I want them to do. I should get rid of them. But I can't afford for them to leave, so I don't fire them." What kind of accountability is this? If they don't have to do what you want them to do, why should they do more than the minimum to keep their job? You've got to make them want to do what *you* want them to do.

So, how do you get people to follow your orders? You're probably an expert on what doesn't work: confusion, threats, lack of trust, bribes, no rules, no rewards, no praise or recognition, no direction, and lack of accountability. So, what is the best way to motivate people to do what you want them to do? **Make people want to do something!** A company-wide system to give people what they want will help you hit your bottom-line goals.

> *Every exceptional employee requires three things:*
> *money, happiness, and motivation.*

Money gives people the basic reason to show up and perform at their minimal level. Money alone will not get them to perform to their maximum ability. **Happiness** at work comes from being motivated. You must provide the **motivation**—this will get people to work with more energy, more effort, and more enthusiasm, and allow them to fulfill their potential, accept responsibility, and become accountable. Many old-school bosses don't offer motivation, praise, recognition, or encouragement. They often say their people continually complain about money. When there's no motivation to do a good job, more pay is the only thing that people can get to help them tolerate a bad situation.

Motivators That Persuade People to Perform

The top motivators to help people become the best they can be:

1. Employees need a **clear understanding of what's expected**
2. Employees need ongoing **praise and recognition**
3. Employees need to **understand the big picture**
4. Employees need to be **appreciated and cared for**

1. To be effective, employees must know exactly what's expected of them. It's pretty hard to stay on course if you don't know where you're going and you don't have a map to get there. I'll talk more about this in a moment.

2. Employees regularly need recognition and praise. O.K., we all throw around "Good job!" to kids when they accomplish something difficult, and it's often used very glibly. But the truth is, we never really grow out of that need to please our parents, people we admire, or our boss. Act as if your people have signs hanging around their necks that say: MAKE ME FEEL IMPORTANT! and SHOW ME THE LOVE!

Provide regular appreciation to everyone you supervise, manage, or lead. People need positive feedback weekly, so make it your priority to recognize at least one person every day. Catch them doing something right and make them feel good about what they do for you! People are like batteries—as they discharge, they need to be recharged at frequent intervals.

Twenty Motivators That Work:

1. Keep a tracking checklist of who you recognize and when.
2. Make sure everyone gets recognized at least every week.
3. Be an inspirational, motivational cheerleader.
4. Start the day with positive encouragement to everyone around you.
5. Being positive makes positive people—it starts with your greeting.
6. Tell employees you appreciate them often:
   a. "I appreciate your efforts . . ."
   b. "You did a good job on . . ."
   c. "Thanks, keep up the . . ."

7. Look for the good in people and appreciate it.
8. Use words that wow!
    a. Three words: "I appreciate you"
    b. Two words: "Thank you"
    c. One word: "[their name]"
    d. Worst letter: "I"
9. Show you care about them, their family, and their future.
10. Ask them their dreams and listen to their personal goals.
11. Tell them the big picture, what's new, good, and bad.
12. Hold company meetings and share the future.
13. Recognize and praise accomplishments in private and in public.
14. Give recognition and time off for extra effort.
15. Give everyone business cards and company shirts.
16. Spend one day per month with the team.
17. Take employees to lunch with you.
18. Give people the tools they need to improve.
19. Provide home computers and e-mail.
20. Spend 33 percent of your time with your people.

You can't learn to ride a bike by watching someone else do it.

Train to Retain

Most small companies hire people with potential and then let them learn on their own by watching others. But most Fortune 500 companies have training systems to ensure they maximize their return on employees. These companies invest in each employee, on average, forty hours of formalized training per year. How much training do your provide? Could you improve your bottom-line by maximizing productivity and eliminating mistakes? You need to train to retain and improve employees.

Training involves doing, not just telling or showing people what to do.
You can't learn to ride a bike by watching others ride. I learned to win sailboat regattas by sailing in lots of races. All the books, lectures, videos, and meetings couldn't teach me the tactics I needed to win. To build an excellent company, training must be ongoing and continuous for everyone.

How to train others

1. Tell them what to do
2. Show them how to do it
3. Let them do it
4. Watch them do it
5. Coach them through it
6. Recognize them
7. Follow up and give feedback

As you train, ask if the employees completely understand. Remember, they really can't do something well until they've done it a few times and you have coached them through the process. Show your key people how you want things done and then let them train their employees. This will elevate their leadership skills and make them accountable and responsible for the end results of their people. Identify what you need to train your people to do and then make these your training topics at least once or twice every year.

Start a training ladder to track your employees' progress. This provides a path for people to become more valuable and to earn more money for you and them. List every task that needs to be learned along the way, a timeline, and minimum standards for each position, then track their progress.

It is best to train every week for at least fifteen minutes. This minimum training program will keep people focused on doing things right. Every month or quarter, provide a half-day training session to cover topics in a more in-depth way. **Remember, training is not an informational meeting or a lecture from the boss. It involves doing the tasks.**

To build a strong company, you need excellent people. You can try to get lucky by hiring and firing people until you get the ones you want. Or you can make people your top priority. You can get your business to work by installing people systems and a training program. The choice is yours!

Chasing Wheelbarrows?

A few years ago I was visiting one of our big job sites. We were building a Kmart store. As I drove out onto the construction site, I noticed one of our long-time laborers cleaning the slab with a broom and shovel. He would sweep debris into his shovel and then walked about 100 yards over to the trash bin. He repeated this for several minutes until I finally asked him: "Where's your wheelbarrow?" He said his boss hadn't given him a wheelbarrow to use. I asked him if a wheelbarrow would make the job go faster. He said that it would. So I asked him why he didn't have one to use. He said his boss wasn't around that morning to get a wheelbarrow for him, so he was doing what he could to stay busy.

So what did I do? I went and looked for the foreman. After looking for a few minutes to no avail, I looked for the job superintendent. He was in the job office in a meeting. So, as the big boss, I went to my truck, got a key to the storage bin, unlocked it, and got a wheelbarrow. I solved the problem! Or did I? *What was wrong with this picture?*

1. The laborer was not trusted with a key to the bin.
2. The laborer was not responsible for:
   - Bottom-line results
   - Using the right tools
   - Thinking
   - Making decisions
   - Doing his best
   - Anything
3. The foreman and superintendent were:
   - Not setting clear targets and goals
   - Not explaining the big picture
   - Not trusting people
   - Not giving up their authority
   - Not training their field crews
   - Not communicating properly

What wheelbarrows do you chase? Why don't people take on more responsibility? In my recent poll of over 2,000 production employees, 66 percent were asked to make decisions. But only 14 percent of them felt empowered and trusted to actually make the decision. They were afraid their boss would yell at them if they made mistakes or the wrong choices. So rather than risk it, employees did as little as they had to. Let me repeat here: **The root of most people problems is the boss, not the employees.**

When the boss owns every problem, only he or she can solve them. When you solve other people's problems for them, your people aren't responsible for any problems. So how can they be responsible for any solutions?

Who makes these decisions, you or your employees?

- Ordering materials
- Scheduling other workers
- Meeting with customers
- Negotiating contracts
- Pricing services and products
- Purchasing equipment or tools
- Choosing suppliers, vendors, or subcontractors
- Hiring employees
- Spending money in excess of $100
- Selecting a coffee brand
- Choosing the paper clips your company orders

Let Go to Grow!

When you continually solve everyone else's problems, your people can't grow or become the best they can be. When you treat employees like children who can't think and don't know any better, they act like children and only do what they're told to do. Each person who works for you wants to be accountable and responsible for some part of his or her job. So it's *your* job to let go and get them doing what you pay them to do. You hire people because you can't do all the work yourself. **But without empowered people, you'll never grow your business beyond what you can control.**

Ask your key people to list the top three priorities they're responsible for accomplishing. I'll bet their answers aren't what you thought they'd be. Most poorly performing people don't know exactly what they're supposed to do and how you want it done.

For example, my field supervisor told me he'd be done with a project in three weeks. Three weeks later I visited the job site to find the project was not final-cleaned or ready for move-in, the job trailer was still on-site, the power was not turned on, and the phones didn't work. I asked him why he wasn't done. He disagreed and said he *was* done. He thought "done" meant calling for the final city inspection. To me, "done" means there is nothing left to do. The problem here was the assumption that "done" means the same thing to everyone. *It doesn't.* Don't assume your people know what you mean unless you explain it clearly, get them to repeat it back, and you both agree.

In order to establish clear expectations, you must take the time to explain exactly what you want, show your employees how to do it, ensure they fully understand the directions, and then reinforce your wishes with coaching and training. As you work on *your* communication problem (yes, if someone doesn't understand what you want, it is YOUR problem, not theirs), and what you want done becomes clear, people will want to take on more responsibility and do more work.

The #1 reason employees don't accept accountability or responsibility is that they don't know exactly what you want them to do. You tell them, but they don't fully understand. So they're afraid to go for it, for fear of their boss's reaction when things aren't done the way he wants.

The number two reason employees don't accept responsibility is that their boss doesn't really trust them to make decisions. Do you tell your people what to do and then say: "Before you do that, check with me first"? Follow this five-step process to get your people to become more accountable and responsible, clearly understand what you want them to do, and feel trusted and empowered to get things done.

Five Steps to Make People Accountable and Responsible

1. Establish Clear Expectations and Understanding

The first and most important step is to make sure people understand what you want them to do. When hired by business owners to visit their company and interview their employees, I always ask each person what the top priorities are for their job and what results they are expected to achieve. In more than two out of three cases, the employees' answers don't match what their boss really wants from them. To ensure that your people know what you want, tell them, show them, and then draw a picture to explain it again. People remember what they see, not what they hear.

Imagine you own a small company that assembles computer workstations. On a special customized rush order from a major customer, you need your production team to assemble, pack, and ship 200 work stations within five days. This will require a change in the normal work flow process to accomplish this intense task. To ensure the order goes out on time, what would you do? Poor managers will jump in themselves, take on their supervisor's job, tell everyone what to do, micromanage every process, and check in with the assembly team every thirty minutes to see if they are on track and doing things the right way.

A good leader would call a team meeting to explain the rush order, outline the goals and deadlines required, and then help the assembly supervisor create a written action plan with the production team's input. The pre-production meeting agenda would include the following:

Seven Steps of Proactive Project Management

1. Identify the project vision

    a.   Review project specifications and requirements

    b.   Explain why the project is important

2. Set clear project targets, goals, deadlines, and milestones

3. Discuss the action plan and alternatives with the whole team

    a.   Get input from production team

4. Write out and present the final written action plan

    a.   Present proactive visual communications

    b.   Review the action plan with your team

    c.   Assign individual team members' responsibilities

    d.   Discuss the timing of each step

    e.   Show team members exactly what's expected

    f.   Visit the production area where the work will take place

    g.   Verify tools, equipment, and materials required

    h.   Address the obstacles or challenges

    i.   Review questions or issues

5. Create a tracking system to measure progress

6. Set up follow-up and review schedules to keep track of progress

7. Celebrate and reward success

2. Create Scorecard and Tracking Systems

In order to make people accountable and responsible, there must be simple milestones and deadlines for them to track. Your team members need to know where they stand in order to meet your goals and expectations. Without a tracking system, people can't be accountable for hitting their expected results without a current knowledge of their progress toward the finish line.

I created a "Hardhat Scorecard" to track the progress of job activities for our project teams. This written tracking system allows them to measure their progress on a daily, weekly, or monthly basis. It includes a place for one HUGE target plus three action-plan goals to track.

Business-Builder Worksheet #18

Hardhat Scorecard

HARDHAT SCORECARD		SCORE:				PROJECT:				
		COMPANY:				TEAM:				
	HOLE #	1	2	3	4	5	6	7	8	
	DATE									
HUGE TARGET		PAR / SCORE	PAR / SCORE	PAR / SCORE	PAR / SCORE	PAR / SCORE	PAR / SCORE	PAR / SCORE	PAR / SCORE	PAR / SCO
GOAL #1		PAR / SCORE	PAR / SCORE	PAR / SCORE	PAR / SCORE	PAR / SCORE	PAR / SCORE	PAR / SCORE	PAR / SCORE	PAR / SCO
GOAL #2		PAR / SCORE	PAR / SCORE	PAR / SCORE	PAR / SCORE	PAR / SCORE	PAR / SCORE	PAR / SCORE	PAR / SCORE	PAR / SCO
GOAL #3		PAR / SCORE	PAR / SCORE	PAR / SCORE	PAR / SCORE	PAR / SCORE	PAR / SCORE	PAR / SCORE	PAR / SCORE	PAR / SCO

	Deadline	Par	Team
My HUGE Target			
Action Step #1			
Action Step #2			
Action Step #3			
Action Step #4			
GOAL #1	Deadline	Par	Team
Action Step #1			
Action Step #2			
Action Step #3			
Action Step #4			
GOAL #2	Deadline	Par	Team
Action Step #1			
Action Step #2			
Action Step #3			
Action Step #4			
GOAL #3	Deadline	Par	Team
Action Step #1			
Action Step #2			
Action Step #3			
Action Step #4			

Hardhat Country Club

Clear Targets ■ Huge Results

SCORECARD

George Hedley, CSP
HARDHAT Presentations
1-800-851-8553 © 2009
www.hardhatpresentations.com
email: gh@hardhatpresentations.com

HARDHAT PRESENTATIONS

At the beginning of each project or production task, get your team together to discuss the major goals you want to track and achieve. Using the previous example of assembling and shipping 200 computer workstations, the **HUGE project target** is to be 100 percent assembled and shipped in five days. The **three project goals** could be to get all materials ready by day one, have the assembly complete by day four, and be shipping-ready by day five. For each project or company goal, decide what targets will keep your team on track, and then review their progress daily, weekly, or monthly to eventually achieve the ultimate goal. This visual tracking system works!

3. Define Levels of Authority

To avoid confusion and misunderstandings, and to build trust with your people, they must clearly know what their level of authority is. Can they buy materials or tools? How much can they spend without approval from their boss? Can they commit the company on contractual issues? Can they hire or fire? What decisions are they authorized to make on their own?

I learned a long time ago that my people make better decisions than I do as the owner of my company. They're more careful with my money than I am. Given clear rules and parameters, your people will become great team leaders and empowered employees. Giving them little or no authority keeps them un-accountable and un-responsible. What's your spending limit for your managers, supervisors, and production employees without having to check with you first? When I increased the maximum spending limit for my field supervisors and project managers to $1,000, they were able to handle most of the day-to-day decisions and issues without my involvement. This allowed them to become fully accountable leaders. My managers know they need two signatures on every contract or purchase greater than $5,000. This allows them to get help or advice on bigger decisions, but keeps projects moving when they need to act fast.

Some other levels of authority for your company might include decisions on purchasing equipment, scheduling employees, supplier or vendor selection, how to handle customer complaints, conflicts with orders and deliveries, hiring, pricing, special customer requests, or delivery issues. When can your production supervisor or manager deviate from the standard procedures? What should happen if an employee needs discipline or termination? Get your managers, supervisors, and production leaders together to discuss all the decisions they have to make to keep their jobs moving. List them, and decide at what point they need to check with their boss before moving ahead.

4. Be a Coach, Not a Controller

People want to be coached, not controlled. The best coach usually wins the most games. When your crew isn't accountable or responsible, it's a reflection of the coach's input, control, or lack thereof. The more you control, the less your people do for themselves. **The more decisions you make for people, the fewer decisions they make for themselves.** The more questions you answer for them every day, the less they have to think and learn. Is that what you want?

Good coaches train their people regularly. Have team meetings to review progress. Ask team leaders to think for themselves and call their own plays. Even great head football coaches don't call their own plays. Your job is to explain what's expected and then provide feedback regarding their progress. Use regular check-in times, follow up, and stay in touch. But don't do it all for them!

Know what else good coaches do? They regularly recognize, praise, and encourage their players to become the best they can be. Make it your priority to look for the good instead of pointing out the bad. Yelling doesn't work. Motivating people makes them want to do more, accept responsibility, and become accountable. The louder you scream, the less they want to do.

5. Celebrate and Reward Success

When accountable and responsible people achieve great results, they need to be thanked and rewarded. It's your job as the leader to set up a fun, competitive, and simple system to reward success. At your regular company, team, or project meetings, pick out several people to recognize for a job well done.

Start a weekly award for the employee or production team player who saves the most money, does something excellent, has the best attitude, makes the best decision, or goes the extra mile for the customer. Keep it fun, challenging, and interactive. Let everyone on the team vote for the winner some weeks, and on alternating weeks let your managers choose the recipient. Give out small prizes like gift certificates to lunch or dinner, tickets to ball games, t-shirts, tools, or happy face stickers.

What Are Your HUGE Priorities?

By now you are well on your way to implementing the seven steps of the Business $uccess Blueprint. You are getting close to owning a business that works without your constant attention. You have created extra time to do what business owners enjoy doing—leading their company and focusing on things that really make a difference.

Ask yourself: *"If I owned a business that worked for me, without me doing all the work, where would I spend my extra time to get the biggest return?"*

_____ Developing an inspiring vision

_____ Setting clear targets and goals

_____ Focusing on financial management

_____ Developing customer relationships

_____ Selling to new customers

_____ Seeking better business opportunities

_____ Motivating and inspiring employees

_____ Training employees

_____ Looking for equity-building ventures

_____ Seeking wealth-building opportunities

Notice that doing the work, managing projects, and supervising people aren't even on the list of what leaders do. Think of great companies, large or small. Excellent companies are run by a boss who takes and makes time to **be the leader instead of a doer**. He or she is the creator, motivator, and seller of the company vision, and what the company offers to its employees and customers. Examples of this leadership style are evident at Microsoft, Dell, Apple, Amazon.com, or GE. When you finally get your company organized, systemized, and making a great profit, it's a lot of fun to be the owner. You work on exciting things, new opportunities, and what really makes a difference. **When you spend time doing all the work instead of leading, your company remains stuck at a level based on how much work you can do and control.**

The Buck Stops Here!

As the leader, you are 100 percent responsible for everything: sales, profits, growth, quality, customer service, organization, people, and management. **Company results are the #1 indicator of your leadership.** Leaders make the necessary leadership decisions to get results they want. Leaders have the courage to change themselves first when things aren't on target. They're on a mission, they try new ideas, change their behavior, change markets, do things differently, innovate, try new methods, and go against the grain.

When I am hired to speak to a company or organization, I always survey the management team and key employees to look for problems and challenges I can help solve. Usually there is an obvious problem that emerges and needs immediate attention. Generally as many as 80 percent of employees rate their company leadership as less than excellent. Very few company owners know how to lead effectively, delegate, trust, motivate, and have a vision that encourages their people to want to follow them. The common denominator to achieve business success is your people—influencing, motivating, and managing them; giving them a vision; getting them committed; and getting them to achieve what you want.

Your employees' output equals your input!

Leaders realize that they get what they expect. When leaders control people or talk down to them, employees are not allowed to be or do their best. Most people perform below their ability because the company leadership needs to be improved. **When you have people problems, it's a reflection on the effectiveness of your leadership.** People don't want to follow the boss. They want to follow the leader. Leaders put people first. They listen, inspire, motivate, care, teach, coach, train, encourage, help, and respect others. Rather than focusing on day-to-day activities, leaders set the vision, set the goals, track targets, and then inspire and motivate their people to follow.

Leaders Are Focused

Today's business leaders are very focused. They have a vision of what they want their company to become, seek the results they want, focus on their people and customers, and constantly innovate and look for new ways to do business. To make their vision become a reality, they spend their time on these five priorities:

Vision   *Clear, inspiring vision, mission, and purpose*

Results   *Set, track, and achieve targets and goals*

People   *Motivate, recognize, appreciate, trust, and coach*

Customers   *Market, sell, serve, seek opportunities and strategic alliances*

Innovation *Change, create, and try new ideas, and work differently*

As a business owner, where do you invest the majority of your time? Are you focused on getting the work done, producing the product, handling the tasks of running your business, or building a business that works? Business-builders are not task- or project-focused. They concentrate on the big picture and what will help their company grow.

When I present my "Effective Leadership" program to companies and at conventions, I give out a short test. It helps determine your leadership style *and where you tend to focus your time and efforts. To take your own leadership test (Business-Builder Worksheet #19) and get your own results, visit:* GetYourBusinessToWork.com/ book.

What's Your Vision?

Effective leaders have an inspiring vision that motivates their people to make big results happen. They set big targets. They focus on their customers. Make people a top priority. And try new and innovative things to take their company to the next level. This gets their people to achieve great results.

Effective leaders stand up and say: "Here's where we're going, and here's how we'll make it happen." Effective leaders have a vision people get excited about, instead of the standard: "Work hard and we'll see how it comes out, and if we do well, maybe you'll get to keep your job and get a small raise or bonus." People get tired of doing the same tasks over and over again without any excitement or passion from their leadership—like digging a long ditch. And when they're done, they just get another ditch to dig. This doesn't make people excited about coming to work and making a difference. **People want to follow someone with passion on a mission.** This gets them excited about doing a better job. Are you a motivator or de-motivator?

Effective leaders start with an exciting vision and then connect it to the specific results they want. Some companies have a vision to be the best company, the best installer, the best consultant, the best store, the best service provider, or provide the best quality. While those are O.K. visions, they're not exciting. Examples of exciting visions:

"We are recognized as the leader in customer service!"

"We are the best at providing engineering to the most difficult technical projects imaginable!"

"We deliver finished products faster than any competitor!"

"We offer value-added services to help customers make more profit!"

What's Your Target?

After defining your exciting vision, specific results must be targeted and quantified. For example, if your vision is to be the best service provider, determine what specific, measurable results would enhance your bottom-line. Some examples of targets include a referral from every customer, only 1 percent mistakes or callbacks, no installation errors, or 98 percent on-time completion. What specific targets and numbers can you shoot for to realize your vision and get the results you want? Without clear targets, your people really don't know what "do quality work" or "be the best" really means.

Ask your employees: "What's our company vision? What specific results are we trying to accomplish? What are our top three priorities?" I'll bet you'll get thirty-seven different answers! To get the results you want, you must get everyone on the same page. Leading and getting results starts with communicating your vision, along with specific targets you expect. Get started now by defining your company vision and specific measurable targets.

Our Vision: _____
Specific Results We Want:

_____

_____

_____

_____

Put People on Your Priority List

When you arrive at the office on Monday morning, what do you do? If you're like me, your tendency is to get right to business and start asking employees questions like: "Did you get that job done?" "What are you going to do first today?" "Did we hit the numbers over the weekend?" "What is on your list this week?" "Are you going to get that sale this week or next?" These type of questions reveal your #1 focus: the job done. Not your people and how you can inspire them to achieve the results you want.

Remember, without productive, happy people, you can't achieve your goals, grow your company, or take any time off. Don't forget to put your people on your priority list. Ask how they are doing every day, how you can help them, and what they need to hit their targets.

Leaders Make Customers a Priority

"I have some deep concerns about the future of your company, the management team you have assembled, and your leadership. Your business is not growing for one reason: you and your management team are not making customer relationships, selling, and creating new revenue a priority."

This is the opening to a letter I sent to a startup company I invested in. I wanted to get them focused on the problem that was causing low profits. Oftentimes, business owners or managers tend to blame bottom-line issues on the economy, competition, the market, or their employees. In reality, top-line and bottom-line results are the biggest indicator of leadership. Making a profit and growing your business is simple. It starts with creating revenue.

No Revenue = No Business = No Profit

Successful leaders are big-time revenue generators who constantly sell. The fastest way to fix a company's profit or growth problems is to generate more revenue. Look at what some of the greatest business leaders say about selling:

"Anyone can manage. Leaders go out and create revenue."
—Sam Walton

"Anyone can mind the store. Revenue takes inspiration and excitement."
—Jack Welch

"Anyone can organize. Leaders cold call and close sales."
—Lee Iacocca

"Anyone can stay busy by selling low price. Leaders create loyal customer relationships and differentiate themselves from competitors."

—George Hedley

For me, selling doesn't come naturally. I don't like to spend my day cold calling potential customers who don't really want to talk to me. Selling is uncomfortable. Selling is not my gift. Several years ago I tried to fix this problem by hiring a salesperson. I figured this would remove me from the sales process. Guess what? It didn't work. He kept asking me to go on sales calls with him. This ticked me off! Now what? **How can you grow your business without selling? You can't!** The leader must carry the sales torch. In my business, clients want to know me, and know that I will be the project leader (not the manager) before they make the decision to hire our company.

The only way you can grow your business is to take personal responsibility for creating customer relationships and profitable revenue. You must be the leader and spend lots of time in sales, customer service, and building customers relationships. You will get the highest return on your time for time spent with customers. What is your personal commitment to selling, marketing, and creating customer relationships? This week? This month? This quarter? This year?

Leaders use personal sales and face-to-face customer meetings as tools for staying in touch with the marketplace. Every breakfast or lunch is an opportunity to be with one of your customers. Every day you can arrange at least one or two meetings with potential and current customers from your target list. Give your management team a weekly progress report to show your commitment to making sales happen.

Remember the startup company I sent the letter to? The CEO finally got on board and made it happen. He made a personal commitment to make ten sales appointments every week. He also committed to personally generating $15 million in revenue within six months. This improved productivity, customer service, and profitability, as he learned to let go and delegate. If your business isn't growing in revenue *and* profits, only you as the leader should be blamed. You live your priorities. Have you made customers and selling a priority?

Get in the Innovation Business

Once you decide to embrace leadership, get out of your "do" role, and let go to grow, you'll find business becomes fun. You have time to innovate, seek better business opportunities, spend time with other visionary business owners, and look for ways to expand your bottom-line. Make it your priority to spend at least 33 to 50 percent of every week focused on activities that will grow your business, improve your people, enhance your management team, build customer relationships, and take your company to the next level. The choice is yours: **LEAD, or die a slow death!**

Step 6: Build People and Leadership Systems!

Business-Builder Action Plans

1. Build a great place to work that attracts and retains the best people.
2. Make finding and training great people a top priority in your company.
3. Motivate people to want to follow you.
4. Give your people what they want: recognition, praise, caring, and a clear picture of their future.
5. Train people to follow the company systems.
6. Make people accountable and responsible.
7. Show your people exactly the results you want.
8. Create a scorecard and tracking system. (Worksheet #18)
9. Determine your leadership style. (Worksheet #19)
10. Develop an inspiring and exciting vision people will want to follow.
11. Constantly change the way you do business by innovation.

To download the Business-Builder Worksheets, visit:
GetYourBusinessToWork.com/book

step **7**

Build Equity and Wealth Systems!

Ask fifty business owners what a perfect business would be like for them and you'll likely get forty-nine different answers. But one common focus will stand out:

Business owners want their business to create equity *and* build wealth!

What does this mean? Well, let's define a few terms so we're all on the same page:

- **PROFIT** is what's left over after all costs, direct and indirect, are deducted from the sales revenue of a business. More formally, it is financial gain resulting from the use of invested capital or equity in a transaction or business. It is the net revenue flowing from a business, property, or investment.

- **EQUITY** is the value of a business, investment, or property net of all amounts owed against it (payables, mortgages, liens, loans or claims). It is the company owner's net stock value in a business or the financial net value of a business. In other words, what the company is worth if the company is closed, all the equipment and fixtures are sold, all the bills and debts are paid, and every amount it is due is collected.

- **WEALTH** is a great quantity or store of money, possessions, property, or other riches. Financial wealth creates passive income that grows in value over the long haul while it reduces debt. It is also defined as *prosperity* and *the condition of being rich or happy.*

Profit creates equity, which allows for building wealth and enjoying the benefits of your business!

If you followed and implemented the ideas of the earlier steps in this book, you should now have an organized and systemized company that is achieving its goals, hitting targets, and making profits. **Your next decision is what to do with your growing equity** that is fueled by increasingly consistent profits. Equity and wealth are the outcome of consistently making profits, and you should be using it to seek other business opportunities, create consistent revenue streams that take care of themselves, and grow your net worth.

Are you becoming a *poor* or *rich* business owner?

Poor Business Owner	Rich Business Owner
Makes all major decisions	Delegates all major decisions
Borrows money	Invests money
Buys equipment and fixtures	Buys rental property
Rents an office, store, or yard	Owns the office, store, *and* yard
Works twelve to twenty hours per day	Works twelve to twenty hours per week
Can't find enough good help	Has great managers and employees

Never has enough time	Spends time on personal priorities
Does all the pricing and purchasing	Seeks opportunities for growth
Lowers price to increase sales	Spends time with loyal customers
Stays at the office or store late	Gets to the golf course early
Is always out of control	Is organized and systemized
Is cash-flow tight	Investments make lots of money
Tells employees what to do	Coaches, motivates, and inspires
Has vendors and subcontractors on speed-dial	Has bankers and investors on speed-dial
Reads orders and contracts	Reads the newspaper's business section
Postpones the dream	Lives the dream every day
Reads *Wall Street Journal*	

Are You Creating Wealth?

As you can see by the definitions above, profit creates equity, which allows for building wealth and finding happiness. To me, wealth includes all things that make you happy. This can be investments, money, family, time, freedom, peace of mind, contentment, enjoyment, success, or owning a business that works for you. Wealth creation can be an outcome of a financially successful business that generates a positive cash-flow and increasing profits. Financial success allows you to enjoy and design your life to do and get what you want. Wealth allows you to make choices about how to spend your time and money. Having no profits, equity, or wealth will keep you stressed out and constantly working to make ends meet.

Wealth is created from assets that make money without you doing much hands-on work. Wealth-building assets create regular positive cash-flow, reduce debt, and are passive instead of needing constant attention and supervision. Liabilities cost money, go down in value, and take a lot of work to get them to pay for themselves. Owning a small industrial building and renting it out is an example of a wealth-building asset. The building creates a net income every month, without much effort or work.

Assets that create wealth go up in value over time, while reducing debt against them. Passive assets can include owning stock in growing and successful public or private companies. Some of the richest people in the world made their money buying Microsoft stock when it was only $10 per share, and then sat back and waited for it to grow in value. I have had the opportunity to invest in many startup companies that have paid off very well. Without any wealth, I couldn't have invested or taken the opportunity to triple or quadruple my money. These investments are passive—I don't have to work at them to make them work.

Owning a business that works without your constant attention, goes up in value, reduces debt, and produces a positive cash-flow and profit can also qualify as a wealth-building asset. Owning a business you have to work at and manage on a regular basis does create equity, but it doesn't qualify as a wealth-building asset. Why not? Because you have to work to keep it working. In addition, your car, equipment, fixtures, and company vehicles are liabilities and not assets because they don't create positive cash-flow, and actually cost money to maintain. Is a tractor an asset? Not unless it works by itself, goes up in value every year, and produces a positive cash-flow without much management.

Wealth-Building Business Opportunities

Equipment rental company	Maintenance company
Business ventures	Material sales
Service contract business	Investments in growing companies
Joint ventures with companies	Investment real estate
Strategic alliances with suppliers	Own stock in private companies
Investment in start-up companies	Own stock in public companies

What Business Are You Really In?

I am asked to speak at fifty or more conventions and meetings every year. After my presentations, people come up to ask questions, give me referrals, and tell me stories that my message triggered. **Many have told me their secret to success: they really made most of their money owning real estate.** Some own their company building or yard, plus the shopping center next door, or a series of homes they rent out, or several warehouse buildings, or they have a partnership interest in a customer's self-storage project. They used their companies to get started, create a positive cashflow, and make a profit. And then, after they had tasted success, they made it their priority to spend only half their time managing their company and the other half investing in wealth-building real estate.

I can't tell you how many clients I have built for who own an oceanfront home plus one or two vacation houses in fantastic places. Every year they want to have meetings two weeks before Christmas to review projects we are building for them. Then they fly off to Aspen or Hawaii for their three-week holiday. And when they return in January, they expected us to have solved all their construction problems and kept on schedule during the holidays. It doesn't seem fair, does it?

As I looked at our situation, I started questioning our business plan as a general contractor. We did more work than our customers, had more employees, took lots of risk, received a one-time contractor's fee for all of our expertise and hard work, had to beg to get paid in full, and didn't make enough money for our efforts. I reflected on the hundreds of buildings we had built for clients who were now living off the ongoing and perpetual monthly rental income these projects produced.

Wealth-Building Real Estate Opportunities

Buy a rental home	Buy another rental home
Buy a residential duplex	Buy an old property and fix it up
Buy an apartment complex	Buy old buildings and upgrade them
Buy your own office building	Build buildings and rent them out
Buy land and subdivide	Build business parks as investments

As an example, the first project I built as a contractor in 1977 was for a business woman who had bought three acres for $150,000. We designed, managed, and built a 50,000-square-foot industrial park for her on the property. Our construction contract was $750,000, and we charged a contractor's fee of $75,000 for overhead and profit to build it for her. Of the $75,000 fee, $50,000 went to cover our company overhead, leaving us a pre-tax net profit of only $25,000. After tax, we ended up with a grand total of $15,000 for seven months of work. Yuck!

Upon completion, the business woman fully leased the project. In her first year, the rent generated a total annual gross income of $240,000, less expenses and mortgage payments of $210,000, thus generating **$30,000 per year** in positive cash-flow. Not great, but better than doing nothing. Ten years later, with increasing rents and inflation, her project generated a positive cash-flow of over **$200,000 per year**. Now her net income is over **$400,000 per year,** and she doesn't even live in the same state! At this rate, why work?

After twenty years as a commercial general contractor, I finally realized why I was in business. Year after year I worked hard to scrape out a 1 to 3 percent pre-tax net profit. I endured lots of stress and took extreme risks building projects for customers who made millions of dollars owning and developing real estate.

Think about your priorities and why you own your business. The purpose of owning your business is not just to serve your customers, manage employees, sell great products, offer unique services, or have a place to go during the day. *You are also in business to make a profit, build equity, seek wealth-building opportunities, and enjoy the benefits of business ownership.* It took me a long time to realize that while our construction company did most of the work, our customers made most of the money. Why? Because I was in the contracting business and

my customers were in the wealth-building business.

Are You a Top 5 Percent or Bottom 95 Percent Business Owner?

Talk to a hundred business owners and follow their progress for ten, twenty, or thirty years, and you will hear the same sad story repeated over and over again. Most work too hard for the effort and risk they take. They never make any real money or have enough left over to invest. They can't stop working and take time off to do what they want. They wish they could start investing some money to get ahead. They can't figure out how to make it get any better.

I notice a lot of small business owners postpone dealing with their financial future until it's too late. They put their long-term goals on hold behind short-term pressures and indulgences (like boats or motor-homes or big equipment that sits in their yard). I have heard the same sad story many times:

Age twenty: "I can't afford to save now. I'm going to school and only work part-time. Maybe in a few years."

Age twenty-five: "I can't afford to save now. I just bought a new pickup truck and I'm thinking about getting married. Maybe later."

Age thirty-five: "I can't afford to invest now. We just had our second child and bought a new house. Maybe after I start my own business."

Age forty-five: "I can't afford investments now. My new business is barely making it and I need to buy some more equipment. My kids will be going to college soon and I'll have to pay their expenses. Maybe after they graduate and get jobs."

Age fifty-five: "I can't afford investments now. I can't get my fifteen-year-old company to make enough money to get ahead. Besides, the economy is tight. And it's probably too late anyway!"

Age sixty-five: "I wish I had started investing sooner. My business has really worn me out. My retirement funds are next to nothing. Maybe it will be better with the Social Security money. I guess I'll keep working as long as I can."

Out of every hundred business owners at age sixty-five, only five or ten will be wealthy or financially secure. Most will still be working in their business because they have to. Others will be broke and depending upon Social Security checks to make ends meet. When you start your business, your goal is to stay in business. After a few years, your goal is to make some profit. Then you finally realize it's not how much you make, it's how much you keep. But you don't make enough to keep enough. So now what?

It's not how much MONEY you MAKE,
it's how much your MONEY MAKES!

Wealthy business owners use money to make more money. Poor business owners work for their money. I find that the more you do, the less you make. **Hard work won't make you wealthy.** Hard work keeps your head down. When your head is focused on work, you can't see opportunities available to you. Remember my slogan:

"You can't get rich with your head in a ditch!"

Get into the Opportunity Business!

So, what business are you in? The answer should be "The opportunity business." In 1994 I made a decision to change our business model and get into the opportunity business, seeking equity and wealth-building opportunities. Our construction company would continue as a general contractor *and* seek real estate investment and development opportunities. We already knew how to build projects, so why couldn't we also participate in the overall development process and profits as well? In order to make this happen, I decided to work differently and spend at least 25 percent of my time seeking wealth-building opportunities. As a contractor on hundreds of commercial, industrial, and office buildings, we were very familiar with the real estate development process. On most projects, we worked closely with the developer and their equity partners, lenders, architects, engineers, real estate brokers, lawyers, escrow officers, title officers, and property managers. As the general contractor, we got our small construction profit while we supervised or coordinated most of the pre-construction and construction work. What are you familiar with to seek wealth-building opportunities?

Build a Wealth-Building Machine!

The key question then becomes: how do you convert your company from what it currently does into a wealth-building machine? The answer is, continue doing what you do well *and dedicate at least 25 percent of your time seeking wealth-building investment opportunities.*

My first investment was small. I put $5,000 down and bought a residential duplex for $40,000 in the low-income part of town. I fixed it up myself and then raised the rent. This allowed me to get a higher appraised value than what I had purchased the property for. I refinanced it and got a new loan, which generated extra cash. With this, I purchased another duplex and did it again. A year later I sold these two properties and bought a sixteen-unit apartment. Following my proven formula, I fixed it up, raised the rents, and then refinanced it. This again generated cash for me to reinvest into other assets.

A small start in low-cost residential real estate will allow you to build wealth and start buying, investing, and developing more assets. **When you own a few wealth-building investments, you start looking at your business differently.** You change your priorities and stop working so many hours for customers and start working on building for your future as well.

Today I only work about eight hours per week in my construction business, and another eight to twelve hours on my investments. (I spend the rest of my business hours doing what I love to do: helping business owners reach their goals, through speaking, consulting, and writing.) You can learn how to convert your company into a wealth-building machine, too. By starting with a small investment, I learned the ropes: how to use invest money wisely and make good decisions. I also learned that by building relationships with bankers, I could leverage money and grow my wealth even faster. Today we own and manage over 500,000 square feet of commercial buildings with over 300 tenants. These properties generate lots of rent and positive cash-flow, and they increase in value nearly every year. Getting started is the key. Don't wait until it's too late! It's never the perfect time. Remember my first client? With only one project she retired with $400,000 in net annual income.

Get Started Building Wealth for Yourself

Make a decision to do more than work on your business. Now is the time to start creating equity and building wealth. Make it a priority to seek wealth-building opportunities. Do whatever it takes. When I started seeking real estate investments, I didn't know how to find property, finance it, manage it, value it, or sell it. But with a clear focus on my future instead of just working for customers, I began to learn how to seek, create, and build wealth.

When I explain real estate financing and joint venture partnership structures to attendees of my Profit-Builder Circles boot camps, they're afraid and don't know where to start. **It's easy to continue to do what you're comfortable doing—running your business.** But to become truly successful, you must start your wealth-building program sooner rather than later.

> **Make it your goal to seek one wealth-building asset within the next six months.**

Call up your banker, a real estate broker, or one of your customers who owns several investments, and take them to lunch. Ask lots of questions. Go to a class or seminar on investing. Buy a book on investments. Get started small. Learn how to make your money work for you. Seek investors, lenders, consultants, and brokers whom you can trust and build a successful team with.

Start by deciding which type of investment you are most comfortable with. I have built a lot of multi-tenant industrial parks for customers. My first large venture into wealth-building investments was to find an old industrial building and fix it up, because that was the type of project we were comfortable with. I knew how to build, upgrade, and remodel buildings, and it was easy to attract friends to invest with me. I found a real estate broker who specialized in older industrial buildings and asked him to present me with opportunities. I offered him ownership for his efforts. Today, twelve years later, the project is fully leased and pays out a hefty monthly cash-flow to me and my investment partners.

The best time to start working on your future and get your finances in order is now! **The best time to start a savings and investment plan is now!** Make a list of what you would like to own in your wealth-building portfolio over the next ten years. You don't have to own 100 percent of every investment. **Ten percent of something is better than 100 percent of nothing**. For example, think like this:

My Ten-Year Wealth Building Plan

Keep 10 percent for myself and find investors and lenders for 90 percent of investment.

Personally invest $100,000 per year equity	= $100,000 / year
Investors and financing contributions	@ $900,000 / year
Total investment value	= $1,000,000 / year
One investment / year for ten years	× 10 investments for 10 years
Total current value after ten years	= $10,000,000 for 10 years
Value with appreciation @ 4% / year compounded	= $14,802,443
Annual cash-flow @ 12% return on investment	= $1,776,293
My personal annual net cash-flow @ 10% ownership	= $177,293 / year
My personal investment equity after ten years	= $1,480,244

Sound good to you? If $100,000 is too much for you to invest, start with less. If you can scrape together only $50,000 per year and invest it wisely, your goal should be to create $75,000 per year net passive income for yourself in ten years. You can make this a reality by starting with a vision of your future and what you want to create in ten or twenty years.

Seek Value-Added Property

We purchased a 24,000-square-foot well-located warehouse building for $1,250,000. It needed lots of refurbishment and a new tenant. Between me and some friends, we invested $250,000 in cash equity and got a $1,250,000 loan from the bank to buy the property. We spent $250,000 upgrading and maintaining the building during the refurbishment, and then leased it to an excellent company at a higher lease rate. Today we enjoy great monthly net cash-flow, and have been offered over $2,500,000 from potential buyers who want to purchase our building. It's not for sale because it will continue to grow in value and generate increasingly higher monthly cash-flow for us owners. Simple!

Joint Venture with Customers and Vendors

Another type of win-win you can seek is joint ventures and strategic alliances with your customers, suppliers, and vendors. Rather than just selling them products, buying from them, or providing services for them, think about how you can partner with them. Consider what you can offer to your customers, vendors, subcontractors, or competitors. Obviously you can offer some of your equity as an investment. But you can also offer your expertise, distribution channels, location, contacts, customer base, sales force, engineering talent, management skills, excess line of credit, financial strength, or banking connections.

For example, I was asked to invest in and be on the board of directors for a small workforce management call center software startup company. They needed my management expertise and wanted strong board members to attract additional investors. To get the software designed faster, they joint-ventured the software development with an engineering company to create the finished product. To expand their customer base, they formed a partnership with a European company to handle sales and service for all of Europe. To expand their sales in the United States, they solicited partnership agreements with major software suite providers in all parts of the country. To generate more cash to grow the company, some new board members were solicited who could provide loans to the company in exchange for stock ownership.

As you can see, there are many ways to invest in your future and generate wealth. The old-fashioned way of doing everything yourself, working hard, and using your own money isn't always the fastest way to grow your net worth and cash-flow. **What can you offer to your customers, vendors, suppliers, or competitors?** What expertise, skills, or talent do you have that can add value to a venture? What sales team, distribution channels, customer base, contacts, or locations does your company have that would add value to another company, product, or service? Do you have excess capital, financial strength, banking contacts, or credit that would add to a new venture?

Think opportunity. And think about how you can leverage what else you've got to offer. My company is now looking for ways to take both construction and financial risk. This allows us to share in the eventual profits of projects. For example, one of our customers asked us to be the general contractor on a project. I asked him if he had all the equity and financial strength needed to complete the development transaction. He said he was investing $400,000 himself but still needed another $400,000 to put the deal together, and he needed a co-borrower to obtain financing. I offered to provide the additional $400,000 equity and signed on the loan for 50 percent of the project ownership and profits. (Note: I didn't agree to put up $400,000 of my money. I agreed to provide $400,000 via my resources *and* other investors.)

This joint venture arrangement provided us with a $4 million construction job plus 50 percent of the overall project development profit. I funded our $400,000 equity investment partly from our construction fee, plus $100,000 of my money, and got the balance from a few friends who were looking for somewhere to invest their money. As a contractor, our fee for overhead and profit was $220,000. But as a developer, we made another $400,000 from our investment. An easy way to triple your return on energy!

Invest in Real Estate to Build Your "REAL" Estate!

Real estate is an interesting word that describes exactly how to build your wealth. **Own some "REAL" property to build your "ESTATE" clearly describes the way to real wealth.** As I mentioned earlier, I started investing in real estate in a small way by buying a residential duplex for $40,000, upgrading it, and then raising the rent. This created additional property value and a positive cash-flow. Another real estate investment I did while building my business was to buy my own building for my company. Getting started with small real estate projects reduces the fear of the unknown. You learn how to work with real estate brokers, find property, make an offer, go to escrow, get a loan, review documents, close escrow, lease out space, hire property managers, negotiate, and do everything else that successful real estate investors do every day.

Every real estate investment has a team of professionals who contribute to the overall success of the project. As a contractor, I know how to hire an architect, go to the city to obtain the required permits, and build the project. But I didn't know much about real estate contracts, making an offer, finding a construction loan, or putting a project budget and pro-forma together, which would calculate whether the project made financial sense. Not knowing how to do some of the parts of the project held me back from moving forward on my plan to start a real estate investment portfolio. What is holding you back from moving forward?

The Real Estate Development Project Team

Developer	Equity investors
Real estate broker	Mortgage broker
Lender	Real estate attorney
Architect	Engineers
General contractor	Subcontractors
Escrow company	Title company
Property manager	Real estate lawyer

What part of the team do you need the most help with? You are probably working with friends or customers who have lenders, brokers, attorneys, title companies, and escrow officers they can recommend. Get their names and go meet them. Ask questions and learn. These resources are the best place to start building your team. Ask for referrals to professionals who specialize in the types of project you want to pursue.

Start Small, But Start!

In order to get started finding a good real estate investment or development project, you've got to find the right property for you. The most important person on the project team is the developer. The developer has a business goal to find a certain type of property to purchase, in a general location, within finite financial parameters. What kind of investment real estate property do you want to start with? Get started by deciding what you want to own, where, and your financial capacity to make it happen.

Business-Builder Worksheet #20

My Personal Real Estate Investment Goals & Objectives

Date I want to own a real estate investment by:

Property type:

Property condition desired:

General location:

Upside potential:

Amount of equity I have available to invest:

My borrowing capacity:

Financing available for this type of property:

Minimum financial return desired:

Cash Is King!

You can't buy real estate without some cash. Make sure you have equity investors lined up and ready to write checks. The most important part of any real estate project team is getting the money together. Generally you'll need between 20 and 35 percent cash equity in every property you purchase. Most lenders will finance between 65 and 80 percent of the appraised value (not the purchase price). The appraised value is based on what the property is worth after you purchase it, improve it, and lease it out at market rate. If you buy a property with the intention of remodeling it, the appraised value will be based on what the upgraded property will generate in rent upon completion. In the example below, the appraised value is based on the new rents the project will generate after completion and the property is fully leased.

Value-Added Real Estate Budget

Before Remodel and Upgrade

Current annual gross income	$50,000 before expenses
Current annual net operating income (NOI)	$40,000 after expenses before mortgage
Capitalization rate (cap rate)	8% varies based on market conditions
Current property value	$500,000 (NOI / cap rate)
Purchase price	$500,000
Remodeling costs	$75,000
Financing and closing costs	$25,000
Total completed project costs	$600,000
Equity cash investment, 25% of costs	$150,000
Permanent loan @ 75% of costs	$450,000

After Remodel and Upgrade

New anticipated gross annual income	$67,500; 35% increase before expenses
New net annual rental income (NOI)	$57,500 after expenses before mortgage
Less annual mortgage @ 8% for 30 yrs.	$39,620
Net annual positive cash-flow	$15,880
Annual return on equity investment	10.4%
New property value after upgrades	$718,750 @ 8% cap rate on new NOI
Property value increase after upgrades	$118,750; 19.8% increase in value

Share the Wealth

A good way to get started is to find equity investment partners who trust you and will co-invest cash into your projects or business ventures. Split the ownership with them based on who provides what percentage of the total equity investment. The developer or managing partner should get a working or promotional interest in the project or business venture from 10 to 50 percent based on the complexity, risk, and potential. And the investors or limited partners should get the balance for providing the needed investment equity capital. A typical ownership split might work like this:

	Equity Investment	Ownership
Developer / Managing Partner	$0	25%
Investors / Limited Partners	$137,500	75%

In the example above, the developer or managing partner gets 25 percent ownership and profit sharing for finding, creating, and doing the work of managing the project. The investors get 75 percent ownership for providing all the equity capital required. The developer should always invest and provide some of the cash equity and share in the investor portion of ownership as well. As an incentive to induce investors to invest in your project, all the equity investment must be paid back before any profit sharing starts. Also offer the investors a preferred return of 8 to 10 percent on their investment before any profit sharing is distributed.

A Good Deal

After identifying what type of investment, real estate property, or business venture you want to acquire, the next step is to find it. Seek out the best real estate or business broker in the market who specializes in the kind of property or business you want to buy. Never ask a residential broker to find industrial property. Hire an expert who can assist you throughout the transaction from acquisition, feasibility, escrow, and financing through leasing or sales.

The best way to find a good real estate broker is to drive to the areas where the property types you are looking for exist. Look at the real estate signs and the brokers who are offering property for sale or lease. Call their offices and ask for the sales manager. Explain what you are looking for and ask who would be the best broker in their office to assist in your search. Next, interview at least three brokers. All of them will tell you they specialize in every type of project, so be slow to choose the right one for your team. Select the professional who is an expert in the building type you desire and can offer the most complete services. For example, if you don't know where to find a loan, make sure they have a relationship with several bankers. If you are weak on calculating a financial feasibility for your investment, select an experienced broker who can do that for you. If you don't know the comparable rents in the area, make sure your broker can provide that for you as well.

Find a Lending Lender

Having a great banking relationship will make you lots of money. Make it a priority to find a banker who will work with you on your investments and real estate projects. Banks are in the business of making loans. They have specialists who are experts in most types of properties, projects, businesses, or investments. Your challenge is to go out and find the one who understands your financial goals and will help your reach your dream.

Make those phone calls and go see several bankers until you find the right one who you can trust to provide the financing you need.

The development and investment process is challenging but financially rewarding. It takes determination and a commitment to reach the finish line and meet your financial goals. The actual process requires steady forward momentum toward a finished project, a fully leased-up investment property, or successful business venture. The good news is that it doesn't take lots of people or time to make your goals become real. You can hire most of the team members needed to do the tasks required. Review the development process below and determine what things you can do yourself and where you need a professional to work for you.

The Real Estate Development Process

> Determine investment goals and objectives
> Select real estate broker
> Identify site or property
> Prepare feasibility study, budget, and investment pro-forma
> Make offer and execute purchase agreement
> Open escrow, perform due diligence
> Obtain investors and equity partners
> Select architect and engineers
> Prepare conceptual project plan, site plan, and preliminary design
> Obtain city approvals
> Secure construction lender and financing
> Prepare final architecture and engineering plans
> Obtain construction bids and award contract
> Construction phase
> Occupancy, leasing or sales
> Obtain permanent financing
> Asset and property management

Finding, purchasing, developing, creating, managing, and owning real estate investment property or other business ventures is the most fun you can have at the office. You can do it part time while managing your regular business. The more real estate you own or businesses you invest in, however, the more you want to own as you see your cash-flow and financial statement grow every year. Take a look at your time management. How can you get a better return on your time? Try getting into the wealth-building business and you will see what a real return on your time can be!

Get in the Game!

I just got off the phone with Susan, the frustrated wife and partner of a swimming pool construction company. She runs the office and does the books, and her husband and son build the pools. She has been preaching to them for years that they aren't making enough money to ever stop working and someday retire. They continue to work hard and often build pools for less than they cost. They are happy staying busy, working with their hands, and paying a premium to use the best subcontractors to build quality pools. But they aren't able to charge a premium for their excellence and get ahead. Why? They aren't focused on their family's future, and they don't have a written plan to reach their long term goals.

What do you want your future to be?

How long do you want to keep working?

Continue to work the same way and you'll never reach your dreams. Start thinking about building wealth. Look for investments that will build a sound future for you, your company, and your family.

Perhaps owning and investing in real estate isn't your thing. Take the same approach, but look for other business opportunities to invest in. Andy, a commercial electrical contractor who attended my Profit-Builder Circle boot camp, left with the idea to get involved with electrical maintenance as a supplement to his low-margin contracting business. Maintenance businesses provide continuous monthly cash-flow and are not dependent on winning job after job to keep your doors open. While looking for ideas and opportunities he found Johnny's Electric, a small service electrical company. Johnny's already had some small maintenance accounts servicing property managers. Andy approached him and made an offer to joint venture a new business together. With Andy's financial strength and expertise in marketing and selling, combined with Johnny's field expertise, the two companies could work together to build a major service company. They agreed to join forces.

The new venture started by offering annual service agreements to property owners and managers to change the bulbs on tall parking lot pole lights for major retail stores, malls, shopping centers, and office buildings. And now, with the focus on "going green," their company changes old, inefficient lights to energy-saving fixtures as a part of their service. As their business grew, they also began putting up holiday lights for the properties they service. Three years later, this business has grown to over $2 million in annual revenue and returns over $600,000 net profit to the owners. The best part? The owners have a general manager who runs the business. This is creative wealth-building at its best!

What can you leverage to start building your future today? What expertise or strength does your business have that you are not using to its fullest potential? Continue to do work the same way and you will continue to make a small profit. But if you are creative and open to trying new things, taking some risk, and investing your time and money in wealth-building ventures, it will lead to a strong financial future.

Step 7: Build Equity and Wealth Systems!

Business-Builder Action Plans

1. Decide to make building your net worth and wealth a part of your everyday business plan.
2. Stop working like a poor business owner and become a rich business owner.
3. Get your money to work for you.
4. Spend 25 percent of your time building wealth and seeking investments.
5. Secure one wealth-building investment opportunity within the next six months.
6. Complete your Personal Real Estate Investment Goals and Objectives. (Worksheet #20)
7. Keep your eyes open for value-added investments and joint venture opportunities.
8. Find investors who will trust you with their cash.
9. Find a lender who will lend you money to build your future.

To download the Business-Builder Worksheets, visit:
GetYourBusinessToWork.com/book

Bonus Step:
Now Enjoy the Benefits!

Select the reason you think most people go into business:

_____ They like to work eighty hours per week

_____ They like to be stressed out

_____ They like to be out of control

_____ They like to be underpaid

_____ They like to be overworked

_____ They like to have no life

_____ They like cutthroat competition

_____ They like to manage employees

_____ They like to deal with other contractors

_____ They like the freedom of business ownership

The #1 reason entrepreneurs go into business is freedom. Freedom from working for someone else. Freedom to do business as they please. Freedom to say no to bad customers, jobs, employees, or contracts. And the freedom to go to work if and when they want! Many business owners complain about working too many hours. While speaking at several industry conventions, I surveyed attendees about their work habits. How do you compare?

Typical business owner work week:

- **15% work 40 hours or less / week**
- **50% work 40 to 60 hours / week**
- **35% work over 60 hours / week**

Unfortunately, the forty-hour work week isn't the norm for today's business owners. The average Fortune 500 company executive works between fifty and sixty hours per week. For those of you who are working more and more and enjoying it less and less, consider these questions:

- *Does earning a living give you time to do any living?*
- *Do you ever stop and wish it would get better?*
- *Are you too busy working to make any money?*

Are you living to work or working to live?

When I talk to business owners, most say they aren't happy with their company, employees, customers, or financial results. Yet they stay in business and keep doing what they know how to do because they don't know what else to do, how to fix it, and can't afford to try anything else. They say: "I can't afford to quit and do what I really would like to." "I can't get my business to work. I'll just keep working harder and maybe it'll get better someday." "What else would I do with my time, if I didn't work so many hours?" I like to say that **business owners become comfortable being uncomfortable!** They get used to the pain.

Life is an adventure! Life is a journey! Life is exciting! Life's opportunities are infinite! An On-Purpose . . . On-Target life only leaves one dilemma: how to do everything you want before you run out of time. There are so many choices and decisions to make in your lifetime that lead you in one way or another and shape your future. Many times you get pulled off course by your business, customers, subcontractors, suppliers, employees, family, friends, and life's crazy circumstances. You end up taking paths you didn't choose.

> **Life's Challenge: Choose to manage your life or let life manage you!**

Choose to control your business, or let your business control you!

Is your problem a lack of time or direction? Only you are responsible for you! You only get one life to live. Do what you want to do first, not last, as unimportant things, challenges, commitments, and your busy life tend to get in the way! Business owners who live On-Purpose . . . On-Target lives have written plans and balanced goals. They know where they're going, why they do what they do, what they want to get involved with, and when to say no. They enjoy every day, have enough time, have well-selected friends, and make their priorities happen.

Stay on Course!

I used to race my sixteen-foot Hobie Cat catamaran sailboat nearly every summer weekend. The big race I enjoyed was the San Luis Wind Bash. The wind really howled for that regatta! My brother crewed for me and together we weighed over 400 pounds (the minimum weight was 250). This gave us a lot of ballast to keep the wind from tipping over the sailboat. My job as captain was strategy, controlling the main sail, steering, and locking the rudders in place (they pop up when they hit floating objects). My brother's job was trimming the front jib sail and balancing the boat.

One year, after two races, we had placed third and first, with the final race to go. As we rounded the fifth and final mark in the last race, we were leading by five boat lengths. The strong wind continued to push us further ahead toward the finish line. With 300 yards to go, we were flying, hiked out on trapeze lines, and leading by fifteen boat lengths. Suddenly our rudders snapped, unlocked, and popped up. The boat made a quick upwind turn off course and slowly drifted to a stop as we flew back into the boat in total disarray. We scurried about, securing the rudders, trimming the sails, and paddling until the boat slowly began moving again. With a little luck we got back to full speed just ahead of the trailing boats and cut across the finish line in first place by only two boat lengths. WOW, a victory!

Racing a Hobie Cat is a lot like owning a business. You know your target—to get to the final destination and cross the finish line. Rudders, like goals and targets, keep you on course and headed in a straight line. It doesn't take much to knock you off track and force you to slow down and drift. Well-defined goals allow you to re-adjust back toward your target when you get off course. Imagine a contractor setting out to build a project without blueprints, specifications, or plans. It would be impossible to build it exactly as the owner dreamed it. Without a precise set of working drawings or written plans with clearly identified targets and specifications, you'll get off track and never hit your goals.

Live More, Give More, and Get More!

Several years ago, I went to a goals seminar to get control of my business and personal life. The following Monday morning, I got to work early and made a list of things to do. Then, after a full day of putting out fires, several panicked phone calls, faxes, e-mails, interruptions, and an emergency conference with a job site superintendent, I hadn't done one thing on my list! At 4:00 p.m., my best customer called and invited me to play golf the next morning to discuss signing a big contract. I didn't have time to play golf with my best customer! I had forgotten my focus. I couldn't even remember my priorities.

A business that works is On-Purpose . . . On-Target, according to the owner's priorities. What will make your business On-Purpose . . . On-Target for you? I want my business to always make a profit, create repeat loyal customers, be 100 percent run by my management team, grow my equity, create wealth, and allow me the freedom to enjoy the six Fs: family, friends, faith, finances, freedom, and fun.

Mike is a friend of mine who owns a medical manufacturing company. He asked if we could meet to discuss his management style. He told me he wasn't reaching his personal goals and wanted to have more time off from work. I asked him to be more specific. He admitted, "I would just love it if I could have at least four hours off on Sundays!"

Prioritize and commit!

Everyone is in a different place. But to get what you want, start by being specific about how you will balance your business and personal goals. Make a commitment and say, "I will leave the office at 5:00 p.m." "I will not check my e-mails or voicemail from 5:00 p.m. until 7:00 a.m." "I will not get involved in decisions my managers or key employees are authorized to make." "I will take a three- or four-day weekend off every month." Be ruthless. Stick to your priorities and get what you want out of your business to enhance your life.

Resolve Every Day To:

- **Focus on your personal and business priorities.**
- **Make progress toward achieving your balanced life goals.**
- **Not postpone your life and family for business pressures.**
- **Live your priorities to get what you want.**

Putting your priorities first is tough. Each day of your life involves difficult demands and tradeoffs. To be On-Purpose . . . On-Target, you must be ruthless about your decisions, choices, commitments, and priorities.

The Three Rs for Living Life On-Purpose . . . On-Target

- **Accept Responsibility**
- **Accept Reality**
- **Accept Risk**

Accept Responsibility!

The following responses to circumstances have become the norm in today's society:

- *"It's not my fault."*
- *"It's just not fair."*
- *"It's not my job."*

When business owners, entrepreneurs, and winners take on a job, they get it done. Period. No excuses. No rules. No reasons why not. Need I say more?

Accept Reality!

Sitting and waiting for "it" to change is counterproductive to living On-Purpose . . . On-Target. Accept your current situation as it is. You can't change the past! However, **you *can* change your future—starting NOW!** Get on with it. Go for it. Make the best of what you've got and make tomorrow even better. Start making those slow but steady changes in how you manage your life. You can do it!

Accept Risk!

Most successful businesses were started by individuals who had clearly defined vision, purpose, and goals. The definition of an entrepreneur is one who "assumes the risk" in a business in expectation of earning a profit. Step up and step out in both your professional and personal life. Take a stand. Take a risk. Act like an entrepreneur. Expect the best and become the best! Take that first step to get what you want. Yes, the first step is often the hardest. I encourage people in this predicament to ask themselves: "What am I waiting for? What's the worst that can happen?" If you never try, you'll never achieve.

Falling Down

As a youngster, my dad often took me skiing in the local mountains. I'll never forget his instructions as I watched expert skiers racing quickly down the slopes with perfect form and parallel turns. He'd say, "You'll never get better standing there watching and wishing you could ski like they can." With that, I would take off and ski down the mountain as fast as I could. My goal was to fall down on every run. This way I knew I was pushing it to the max. **You don't get better if you don't fall down often.** You get better when you try new tricks and techniques. What new tricks have you tried in your business lately to make it better, to make more profit, or to start hitting your long-term goals?

Have you ever noticed that successful people always get up when they fall down? And the really successful ones fall down a lot! Stay alert. Watch for opportunities. Be quick to change. Make your own luck. Always be ready and well prepared. Know where you want to go and let others know where you want to go, too. Ask others how they did it. Seek advice. Stay informed. Keep improving. Stay on top of your field. And always go for it!

Give to the world the best you have,
and the best will come back to you.

Have you ever noticed that successful people who have their lives in order are also more active, involved, and generous with charities, their church, and volunteer organizations? They make giving back a top priority in their lives. Your success is an result of how much you do for others. Your deeds have lasting impact, not your stuff, power, position, or busy schedule. Successful people make more time to serve others. Becoming a success is directly proportional to what you give. It's a fine line—some people give to get—but that won't work for most.

What you GET is a RESULT of what you GIVE!

I receive an overwhelming return on my investment every time I give my time, talent, and money. Giving is the outward expression of your inner commitment, character, and dedication. There is a direct conduit between your heart and your wallet. A banker once told me that the first line he looks at on a loan applicant's tax return is "contributions." He tells me he can usually judge a person's true integrity and sincerity by looking at that one single entry. People who donate money generously and on a regular basis can be trusted. People who don't find time or money to give to others are self-centered, and won't get everything they want in life. People who don't give are the only ones who complain about giving. **Give giving a try.** I guarantee you will get more in return than you ever give.

> *"Only a life lived for others is worthwhile."*
> *—Albert Einstein.*

I started my business with the slogan: "Do a good job for the customer and the money will come." Putting others first always works in both business and life. So go out and give, get, grow, and enjoy what you've got!

Time Off for Good Behavior?

I always dreamed of taking lots of vacations as a reward for owning my business, taking a risk, and working so hard. This seemed impossible while building my company. My mistake was thinking I had to do everything myself and make every big decision. I didn't trust my people enough. But later, I realized I wasn't really as important or as smart as I thought I was. I tried an experiment and took a ten-day vacation without calling the office or checking e-mail. When I got back, I discovered that my managers had actually done a better job than I would have if I'd stayed at the office and continued to micromanage them! That was when I realized that my management style was the problem with my employees.

My survey of business company owners indicates that 65 percent take less than two weeks of vacation annually. They must also think they're too important to leave their company to their employees to manage for a few days. Only 35 percent realize that time off is good for both their business and personal life. How do you compare?

Business owner vacation days per year:

- *10% take 0 to 5 days*
- *50% take 6 to 10 days*
- *20% take 11 to 14 days*
- *10% take 15 to 20 days*
- *10% take over 20 days*

I've been a business owner for over thirty years, and I realize the value of time off. When I work too much, I make mistakes, tend to micromanage, make less money, and miss great opportunities. Now, when I head home for the weekend or off on vacation, I have two purposes in mind. First, spend time on family, faith, friends, fitness, or fun. Second, work on bettering my business skills by reading business books or magazines on topics where I need to improve. When I come back to the office, my mind has been focused on solving problems or seeking opportunities. I am filled with new ideas, and refreshed and excited about the future.

Be Free!

The choice of how to spend your time is yours. Put your priorities first and reap the real rewards of business ownership. Make a commitment to put yourself, your spouse, your family, and your future first. That will be the best decision you make today and tomorrow. **Successful entrepreneurs don't do the work. They act and think like leaders**. As a result, they have lots of time to enjoy the benefits of a business that works for them. Only you can make the reason you went into business become a reality:

FREEDOM!

See you on the links!

Bonus Step: Now Enjoy the Benefits!

Business-Builder Action Plans

1. Start managing your life and stop letting your business control you.
2. Take more time off. You deserve it!
3. Put your six Fs first.
4. Accept responsibility, reality, and risk for the situation your business is in and where it is headed.
5. Give more to get more.

To download the Business-Builder Worksheets, visit:
GetYourBusinessToWork.com/book

About the Author

George Hedley, "The Business Builder," is an entrepreneur, business owner, and the recognized authority on how to build a business that consistently produces bottom-line results, loyal customers, leaders, and profits. He is the author of several books, including *On-Purpose . . . On-Target!* and *The Business Success Blueprint* series. George is also a regular columnist in numerous magazines.

George's expertise is based on his real-world experience of leading people, running a profitable company, and getting things done. He founded and built his major commercial construction and development company, taking it from $0 to $50 million in only seven years! For his accomplishments, George received the nationally recognized "Entrepreneur of the Year" award by Ernst & Young and *Venture* magazine.

George is a graduate of the University of Southern California in Civil Engineering and has served as the president of five industry associations. He plays golf several times a week with his favorite golfing partner, his wife Alana. They live in their cottage in Newport Beach, California.

Today, along with managing his company, George owns Hardhat Presentations and is a popular speaker at companies and associations. He has earned the prestigious "Certified Speaking Professional" designation from the National Speakers Association. His Business-Building Programs cover topics such as Building Leaders, Profits, Customers, and Wealth. He also holds in-depth two-day Profit-Builder Circle Academy boot camps open to business owners who want to get their businesses to work.

Let's Talk About Building Your Business!

Contact George Hedley for information about him speaking to your organization or with your questions or comments. E-mail: **gh@hardhatpresentations.com**

To sign up for George's monthly free **newsletter** visit: **HardhatPresentations.com/signup**

To sign up for more information to attend a **Profit-Builder Circle Academy** visit: **HardhatPresentations.com/profit-builder_circles.asp**

To read George's recent **BLOG** posts visit: **GetYourBusinessToWork.com**

Visit his website and online **bookstore** at: **HardhatPresentations.com**

To download **Business-Builder Worksheets**, visit: **GetYourBusinessToWork.com/book**